A Paines Plough, Wa
and Hull Truck Th

CW00540914

Jumpers for Goalposts

by Tom Wells

The first performance of *Jumpers for Goalposts* took place on
5 April 2013 at Watford Palace Theatre

Jumpers for Goalposts

by Tom Wells

Cast

LUKE	Philip Duguid-McQuillan
VIV	Vivienne Gibbs
GEOFF	Andy Rush
DANNY	Jamie Samuel
JOE	Matt Sutton
ANNOUNCER	James Alexander Gordon

Creative Team

Direction	James Grieve
Design	Lucy Osborne
Lighting Design	Charles Balfour
Sound Design	Nick Manning
Assistant Direction	Mark Maughan
Dialect Coach	Daniele Lydon
Company Stage Manager	Maddie Baylis
Deputy Stage Manager	Alicia White
Rehearsal Assistant Stage Manager	Sally Inch
Assistant Stage Manager	Amy Slater
Production Manager	Matt Ledbury
Costume Supervisor	Mark Jones
Tour Production Manager	Bernd Fauler
Sound Associate	Alex Braithwaite
Set and Costume	Watford Palace Theatre

Paines Plough, Watford Palace Theatre and Hull Truck Theatre would like to thank the following for their support on the production:

LRB Trophies
W Boyes & Co

TOM WELLS (Writer)

Tom is from Kilnsea, East Yorkshire. Plays include: *Jonesy* (nabokov, 2012); *The Kitchen Sink* (Bush Theatre, 2011, winner of the Most Promising Playwright – Critics' Circle, 2011 and the 2012 George Devine Award); *Spacewang* (Hull Truck, 2011); *Me, As A Penguin* (West Yorkshire Playhouse, 2009 and Arcola Theatre/UK tour, 2010); *About A Goth* (Paines Plough/Òran Mór, 2009) and *Notes For First Time Astronauts* (Paines Plough, later at Soho Theatre, 2009). *Ben & Lump,* which Tom wrote as part of the Coming Up season was broadcast on Channel 4 in spring of 2012.

In 2009 Tom was a member of Paines Plough/Channel 4's Future Perfect scheme and in 2012 he was Associate Playwright at Hull Truck. He has been co-commissioned by Hull Truck, Birmingham Rep and Watford Palace and is writing a new play for Radio 4.

PHILIP DUGUID-MCQUILLAN (Luke)

Philip trained at Birmingham School of Acting.

Theatre includes: *The History Boys* (Theatre by the Lake, Keswick); *Execution of Justice* by Emily Mann (Southwark Playhouse); *Punk Rock* by Simon Stephens (Kaleidoscope).

Film includes: *Eliminate: Archie Cookson* (Agent Pictures).

VIVIENNE GIBBS (Viv)

Vivienne trained at LAMDA.

Theatre includes: *Blood Carmen* (Moving Theatre/Théâtre Éphéméride); *The Last Curiosity* (Young Vic workshop); *The Nature of Things* (The Place); *Long Tooth* by Trudi Jackson/Vivienne Gibbs (Gilded Balloon); *Splendour* by Abi Morgan (Cobden Club); *This Property is Condemned, The Lady of Larkspur Lotion* (Occam's Razor); *Elephant Man* (Union Theatre/Sincera Brazil tour); *Mud, La Entrevista* (Arcola); *Martine McCutcheon Needs Me* (Soho Theatre Studio).

Vivienne also performs regularly with the Somerstown mentoring charity, Scene and Heard.

Television includes: *Comedy Lab* (Channel 4).

Film includes: *Act of God* (Giant Films); *Atonement* (Working Title); *Rabbit Fever* (Rabbit Reproductions).

ANDY RUSH (Geoff)

Andy trained at Birmingham School of Acting.

Theatre includes: *The Kitchen Sink* by Tom Wells (Bush); *Hello/Goodbye* by Peter Souter (Hampstead); *Love's Labour's Lost* (The Lamb Players); *Sense* by Anja Hilling (Made by Brick); *Anna Karenina* (Arcola); *Romeo and Juliet* (Cheltenham Everyman).

Television includes: *Holby City*, *Wizards vs Aliens, Casualty* (BBC); *New Tricks* (Wall To Wall Ltd).

Film includes: *Here and Now* (Small But Tall Films Ltd).

JAMIE SAMUEL (Danny)

Jamie trained at ArtsEd School of Acting.

Theatre includes: *The Kitchen Sink* by Tom Wells (Hull Truck); *66 Books, Blanded* by Frazer Flintham (Bush); *Pushing Up Poppies* by Kieran Lynn (Theatre503); *2nd May 1997* by Jack Thorne (Bush/Manchester Royal Exchange); *The English Game* by Richard Bean (Headlong); *The Conservatory* by Mark Dooley (Old Red Lion).

Television includes: *The Promise* (Channel 4/Daybreak Pictures); *A Touch of Frost* (ITV); *Doctors* (BBC); *The Bill* (ITV).

Film includes: *Territory* (50 West Productions).

Short film includes: *Own Worst Enemy* (Grosvenor Television); *The Coward* (Curzon, Soho).

MATT SUTTON (Joe)

Theatre includes: *YPS King Lear* (RSC); *Romeo and Juliet* (Northern Broadsides); *Up on Roof* by Richard Bean (Hull Truck); *The Magic Paintbrush* (West Yorkshire Playhouse); *Steve And Then It Ended* by Adam Usden (Theatre503); *Me & My Friend* by Gillian Plowman (King's Head, Islington); *Night Cellar* (BAC); *Macbeth* (National Youth Theatre).

Television includes: *Emmerdale, Distant Shores, Shakespeare Stories,*

Much Ado About Nothing, *The Taming of the Shrew*, *55 Degrees North*, *FC Dave*, *Cocaine Nation*, *Rum, Sodomy and the Lash*, *The Bill: Beech is Back*, *rForest People*, *Kid's Court*.

Film includes: *Goal 2: Living the Dream*, *Peter*, *How to Film Your Neighbour*, *The Notebooks of Cornelius Crow*, *Mystery Play*.

Radio includes: *Guardian Angel*, *Stories for Another Day*, *Abandoned Projects*, *The Land of Green Ginger*, *King of the Road* (Radio 4); *Writing the City* (Radio 3).

JAMES GRIEVE (Direction)
James is the Joint Artistic Director of Paines Plough. He was formerly co-founder and Artistic Director of nabokov for ten years and Associate Director of the Bush Theatre.

Directing credits for Paines Plough include: *The Sound of Heavy Rain* by Penelope Skinner (as part of the Roundabout Season/Sheffield Theatres); *You Cannot Go Forward From Where You Are Right Now* by David Watson (as part of A Play, a Pie, and a Pint season, Òran Mór/Traverse Theatre, Edinburgh/Manchester Royal Exchange /Belgrade Theatre Coventry); *Wasted* by Kate Tempest (Latitude Festival/ Roundhouse/national tour); *Love, Love, Love* by Mike Bartlett (Royal Court/ Drum Theatre Plymouth/national tour); *Tiny Volcanoes* by Laurence Wilson (Liverpool Everyman/Latitude Festival/ national tour); *Fly Me to the Moon* by Marie Jones (as part of A Play, a Pie, and a Pint season, Òran Mór/Live Theatre, Newcastle/Traverse Theatre, Edinburgh/Belgrade Theatre, Coventry/ Bewley's Café Theatre, Dublin).

Other directing credits include: *The Whisky Taster* by James Graham, *St Petersburg* by Declan Feenan and *Psychogeography* by Lucy Kirkwood (all for the Bush); *Artefacts* by Mike Bartlett (nabokov/Bush/UK tour/59E59, New York).

LUCY OSBORNE (Design)
Theatre credits include: *The Machine* by Matt Charman (Donmar Warehouse/ MIF/Park Avenue Armory, New York); *Hello/Goodbye* by Peter Souter

(Hampstead); *Berenice* and *The Recruiting Officer* (Donmar Warehouse); The Roundabout Season (Paines Plough/Sheffield Theatres); *Huis Clos* (Donmar Season at Trafalgar Studios); *Love, Love, Love* by Mike Bartlett (Paines Plough/Royal Court/Drum Theatre Plymouth); *The Taming of the Shrew* and *Twelfth Night* (for which she won Chicago 'Jeff Award' for Scenic Design; Chicago Shakespeare Theatre); *Plenty*, *The Long and The Short and The Tall*, *The Unthinkable* (Sheffield Theatres); *Precious Little Talent* by Ella Hickson (Trafalgar Studios); *Playhouse Live: Here* (Sky Arts); *Shades* by Alia Bano for the Royal Court's Young Writers Festival; and *When Romeo Met Juliet* (BBC).

Lucy was an Associate Artist at the Bush Theatre and her designs there included *Where's My Seat* by Deirdre Kinahan, Jack Thorne and Tom Wells, *The Aliens* by Annie Baker, *Like A Fishbone* by Anthony Weigh, *The Whisky Taster* by James Graham, *If There Is I Haven't Found It Yet* by Nick Payne, *Wrecks* by Neil LaBute, *Broken Space Festival*, *Sea Wall* by Simon Stephens, *2,000 Feet Away* by Anthony Weigh, *Tinderbox* by Lucy Kirkwood and *the dYsFUnCKshOnalZ!* by Mike Packer.

Lucy trained at the Motley Theatre Design School, having also gained a BA in Fine Art from the University of Newcastle.

CHARLES BALFOUR (Lighting Design)
Charles has been a Freelance Lighting Designer since 1987, working in theatre, dance and opera.

His recent designs include: *The Accrington Pals* and *To Kill a Mockingbird* (Manchester Royal Exchange); *The River* by Jez Butterworth, *Choir Boy* by Tarell Alvin McCraney (Royal Court); *Labyrinth of Love* (Rambert Dance); *Morning* by Simon Stephens (Traverse, Edinburgh /Lyric Hammersmith); *Posh* by Laura Wade (Royal Court at Duke of York's); *Carmen* (Vlaamse Opera); *Run For It* (Scottish Ballet/Cultural Olympiad); *The Guid Sisters* (Royal Lyceum, Edinburgh); *A Kind of Alaska/Krapp's*

Last Tape (Bristol Old Vic) and Crave/Illusions by Sarah Kane/Ivan Viripaev (ATC). Other designs include: Chicken Soup With Barley by Arnold Wesker, Now or Later by Christopher Shinn and The Ugly One by Marius von Mayenburg (Royal Court); The Beauty Queen of Leenane and The Girlfriend Experience by Alecky Blythe (Young Vic); A Doll's House, Oh! What a Lovely War and Who's Afraid of Virginia Woolf (Northern Stage); The Hypochondriac and The Tempest (Liverpool Everyman); The English Game by Richard Bean and Angels in America Parts 1 & 2 (Headlong); The Duchess of Malfi and Hedda Gabler (West Yorkshire Playhouse).

NICK MANNING (Sound Design)
Nick is the Head of Sound at the Lyric Hammersmith.

For the Lyric: Morning by Simon Stephens, The Chair Plays, Saved, 1984, Roald Dahl's Twisted Tales, Dick Whittington and His Cat, The Big Fellah by Richard Bean (also UK tour); A Thousand Stars Explode in the Sky by David Eldridge, Robert Holman and Simon Stephens, Ghost Stories (also Liverpool Playhouse/Duke of York's – Olivier Award nomination for Best Sound Design); Three Sisters, Jack and The Beanstalk, Comedians, The Jitterbug Blitz, Hang On, Cinderella, Spyski!, Depth Charge, Love – The Musical, The Birthday Party, The Resistible Rise of Arturo Ui, Beauty and the Beast, Accidental Heroes, Absolute Beginners, Ramayana, Metamorphosis, Too Close to Home, The Odyssey, Some Girls are Bigger Than Others, The Firework-Maker's Daughter, Don Juan, Oliver Twist, Pericles, Camille, A Christmas Carol, The Prince of Homburg, Aladdin, The Servant and Pinocchio.

Other theatre includes: The Acid Test by Anya Reiss, The Empire by DC Moore (Royal Court); Grumpy Old Women 2, Britt on Britt, Grumpy Old Women (Avalon); Gizmo Love, Excuses, Out of Our Heads (ATC); The Unsinkable Clerk (Network of Stuff); Airsick by Emma Frost, Crooked by Catherine Trieschmann, When You Cure Me by Jack Thorne (Bush); Darwin in Malibu

(Hampstead); Rabbit by Brendan Cowell (Frantic Assembly); Great Expectations (Bristol Old Vic).

Forthcoming productions include: Candida (Theatre Royal Bath).

DANIELE LYDON
(Voice and Dialect)
Daniele trained at Central School of Speech and Drama and has an MA in Voice Studies. Since then, her work includes: Resident Dialect Coach on The Lion King and Billy Elliot (West End); The Paradise (BBC); The Kitchen Sink by Tom Wells (Bush/Hull Truck); Blue Heart Afternoon by Nigel Gearing (Hampstead); The Amazing Dermot (Channel 4). She has also worked with directors Mandani Younis, Tamara Harvey, Richard Beecham and producer Ash Atalla.

MARK MAUGHAN
(Assistant Direction)
Mark is Paines Plough's trainee director. He is studying on the MFA in Theatre Directing at Birkbeck. He was previously an actor as part of the acclaimed Colombian repertory group Teatro La Candelaria. He works as a director for RADA New Writing workshops and the CASA Latin American Theatre Festival. Mark took the Advances in Scriptwriting course with Stephen Jeffreys and worked as an Assistant Director for Live Theatre, Newcastle. Directing credits include: Petrification by Zoe Cooper (GIFT Festival); Longshore Drift (OVNV 24 Hour Plays, Old Vic); Los imbeciles están de testigo, Forgive me for you betraying me, Los hermanos Cuervo (radio and rehearsed readings, CASA); Twelfth Night (associate, LAMDA); As I See It (Jaw Rattle Productions); The Tempest (CAST); Look Back in Anger by John Osborne (CUP); Yellow Moon by David Greig (ADC Elsewhere).

Assisting credits include: Lungs by Duncan Macmillan with Richard Wilson (Paines Plough Roundabout Season); Good With People by David Harrower with George Perrin (Traverse); The Pitman Painters by Lee Hall with Max Roberts (UK tour).

'Revered touring company Paines Plough' *Time Out*

Paines Plough is the UK's national theatre of new plays. We commission and produce the best playwrights and tour their plays far and wide. Whether you're in Liverpool or Lyme Regis, Scarborough or Southampton, a Paines Plough show is coming to a theatre near you soon.

'If new writing in this country is going to have any far-reaching significance, then it needs the touring company Paines Plough.' *Independent*

Paines Plough was formed in 1974 over a pint of Paines bitter in The Plough pub. Since then we've produced more than 100 new productions by world renowned playwrights like Stephen Jeffreys, Abi Morgan, Sarah Kane, Mark Ravenhill, Dennis Kelly and Mike Bartlett. We've toured their plays to hundreds of places from Manchester to Moscow to Maidenhead.

Our Programme 2012 saw us tour 11 productions to 46 towns and cities across the UK.

'That noble company Paines Plough, de facto national theatre of new writing.' *Telegraph*

Supported by
ARTS COUNCIL ENGLAND

Paines Plough are

Joint Artistic Directors	James Grieve
	George Perrin
Producer	Tara Wilkinson
General Manager	Claire Simpson
Assistant Producer	Hanna Streeter
Interim Administrator	Sean Linnen
Production Manager	Bernd Fauler*
Trainee Director	Mark Maughan
Production Assistant (Central School of Speech and Drama Placement)	Tom Pope
Administrative Assistant (Leeds University placement)	Frances Craven
Administrative Assistant (Goldsmiths University placement)	Maria Luisa Vergara
Press Representative	Kate Morley*

*denotes freelance

Board of Directors
Caro Newling (Chair), Christopher Bath, Micaela Boas, Cindy Polemis, Nia Janis, Ola Animashawun, Simon Stephens, Tamara Cizeika, Zarine Kharas.

Contact
Paines Plough, 4th Floor, 43 Aldwych, London, WC2B 4DN
tel +44 (0) 20 7240 4533 fax +44 (0) 20 7240 4534
office@painesplough.com
www.painesplough.com

Follow @PainesPlough on Twitter.com/painesplough
Add Paines Plough on Facebook.com/painesplough

Donate to Paines Plough at justgiving.com/painesplough

Watford
Palace Theatre

Watford Palace Theatre is a local theatre with a national reputation.

The creative hub at the heart of Watford, the Palace engages people through commissioning, creating and presenting high-quality theatre, and developing audiences, artists and communities through exciting opportunities to participate. Contributing to the identity of Watford and Hertfordshire, the Palace enriches people's lives, increases pride in the town, and raises the profile of the area. The beautiful 600-seat Edwardian Palace Theatre is a Grade II-listed building, busy with live performances and film screenings seven days a week, offering world-class art to the tens of thousands of people visiting the Theatre each year.

The quality of work on stage and beyond is central to the Theatre's ethos. Recently, the Palace has enjoyed critical acclaim for its productions of Neil Simon's **Lost in Yonkers**, Charlotte Keatley's **Our Father**, Julian Mitchell's **Family Business**, Gary Owen's **Mrs Reynolds and the Ruffian** (TMA Best New Play nomination) and Neil Simon's **Brighton Beach Memoirs** (TMA Best Supporting Performance in a Play nomination).

The Palace has co-produced a number of acclaimed new plays including **After the Rainfall** by Curious Directive, **Bunny** by Jack Thorne, a Fringe First-winning production in association with nabokov and the Mercury Colchester, **Young Pretender** by E V Crowe, co-produced with nabokov and Hull Truck Theatre in association with Mercury Colchester and **Dusk Rings a Bell** by Stephen Belber, co-produced with Hightide Festival Theatre.

Projects such as **Ballroom of Joys and Sorrows**, **Celebrate Eid**, **Diwali at the Palace**, **Celebrate Vaisakhi** and **Black History Month** have brought together the creativity of Watford's diverse communities. These build on the regular programme of Palace and Hertfordshire County Youth Theatres, adult workshops, backstage tours, community choir and extensive work with schools.

Supported by
ARTS COUNCIL
ENGLAND

Watford Palace Theatre
ON TOUR

Work created at and with Watford Palace Theatre regularly tours nationally. Productions you may have seen recently:

Medea by Mike Bartlett, co-produced with Headlong and Citizens Theatre, Glasgow

After the Rainfall co-produced with Curious Directive and Escalator East to Edinburgh

Tiddler and Other Terrific Tales from the book by Julia Donaldson, co-produced with Scamp, touring nationally in 2012

NowHere choreographed by and co-produced with Divya Kasturi, which has toured nationally

Stickman from the book by Julia Donaldson, co-produced with Scamp, which has toured internationally and played at London's Soho and Sound Theatres and the Edinburgh Festival

Bunny by Jack Thorne, a Fringe First-winning production in association with nabokov and the Mercury Colchester, which has toured nationally and played at London's Soho Theatre and in New York

Family Business, a new play by Julian Mitchell, co-produced with Oxford Playhouse

Street Scene, music by Kurt Weill, book by Elmer Rice, lyrics by Langston Hughes, co-produced with The Opera Group and the Young Vic, which won the Evening Standard Award for Best Musical

Friend or Foe by Michael Morpurgo, co-produced with Scamp Theatre

Britain's Got Bhangra conceived and written by Pravesh Kumar, music by Sumeet Chopra, lyrics by Dougal Irvine, co-produced with Rifco Arts and Warwick Arts Centre

Great Expectations by Charles Dickens, adapted by Tanika Gupta, co-produced with English Touring Theatre

facebook.com/watfordpalace
twitter.com/watfordpalace
www.watfordpalacetheatre.co.uk

Nearly 40 years ago, an advert appeared in *Time Out*: 'Half-formed theatre company seeks other half'. With the caveat that the 'other half' must be willing to move to Hull, **Mike Bradwell** set out to establish one of the most innovative theatre companies in Britain.

Writers and directors such as **Alan Plater** and **Anthony Minghella** joined Hull Truck over the course of the next 12 years. But it was **John Godber** who became the key figure in Hull Truck's next 27 years. Touring his brand of theatre to great acclaim, the company rose to new heights of both popularity and national importance. **Gareth Tudor-Price** joined the company in 2002 and, by encouraging talents such as **Richard Bean** and **Amanda Whittington**, broadened Hull Truck's artistic output still further.

Today, the legacy of both Bradwell and Godber, together with all the artists and writers they have fostered, is the foundation of the company's new home, a brand new theatre, which opened in 2009.

Now the company is responding to the opportunity of an increased capacity across two theatre spaces, an extensive community engagement programme and the exciting journey to discover and develop the next generation of outstanding writers and theatre-makers at Hull Truck Theatre.

New writing is at the core of Hull Truck Theatre's work. It is truly a writers' theatre, with a mission to produce the work of living playwrights and to showcase work made by the very best contemporary theatre-makers.

Recent productions or commissions by **Hull Truck Theatre** include plays by Tom Wells, Tom Wainwright, Lucinda Coxon, Anthony Weigh, Dave Windass, Morgan Sproxton, Richard Vergette, Sarah Davies and Joe Hakim.

In the last few months our collaborators and partners have included **Headlong**, **Rash Dash**, **Bolton Octagon**, **Bristol Old Vic**, **Greyscale**, **Gate Theatre** and **nabokov.**

We invest in today's artists. We celebrate new forms of theatre-making. We make theatre for today's audience.

JUMPERS FOR GOALPOSTS

Tom Wells

Characters

VIV, *thirty-seven*
JOE, *thirty-nine*
BEARDY GEOFF, *twenty-five*
DANNY, *twenty-two*
LUKE, *nineteen*

This text went to press before the end of rehearsals and so may differ slightly from the play as performed.

Week One

VOICE ON RADIO. Man City, 2 – Tranny United, 1. Lesbian
Rovers, 5 – Barely Athletic, 0.

*A changing room in Hull. A bit scruffy. Benches and graffiti.
A bin. Some narrow windows high up on the back wall.*

Showers are through a doorway, offstage.

*JOE, DANNY and LUKE are sitting down, looking a bit
knackered. VIV is fuming.*

*Throughout the scene, everyone apart from LUKE gets
changed out of kit, into clothes. LUKE just puts more clothes
on.*

GEOFF *moonwalks on.*

VIV *glares.* GEOFF *stops.*

VIV. You haven't earned that moonwalk, Beardy, and, deep
down, I think you know it.

JOE. Bit harsh, Viv.

VIV. Oh is it? Very good.

JOE. He did score.

VIV. For the wrong team, Joe. The wrong fucking –

GEOFF. Still a goal.

VIV. Yes, a goal that plunged us from a respectable four-nil
defeat where people go 'never mind, Viv, we all have an off-
day', to a humiliating five-nil defeat where people actually
take you to one side and go: 'Viv, have you considered
badminton?'

DANNY. Have you considered badminton?

VIV. Shameful. It is.

But that, that right, that is just a drop in the ocean of of of, incompetence on display by you lot today. All of you. Including me.

VIV *rummages in her bag for a notepad.*

I've made notes.

VIV *picks up a football.*

Right, Luke. What's this?

VIV *points at the football.*

LUKE. Sorry?

VIV. This. What is it?

LUKE. Um. Football?

VIV *gives him the football.*

VIV. I'll let that sink in.

LUKE *looks at the football.*

DANNY. Viv.

LUKE. No it's. Good isn't it? Start with the, the basics.

VIV. Joe love. I know your life's a steaming pile of shit at the moment, properly shit and it will be for, for a while and, this probably isn't your top priority but, thing is: you do need to work on your fitness. We'll go jogging. We'll start tomorrow.

JOE. Maybe.

VIV. Good. Two things, Danny: one: you're always playing football, I remember you being really good at it. You're not, you're shit. What's happened? Two: thought you're doing a course. Coaching and that.

DANNY. I am.

VIV. Where's the fucking, coaching then? Guidance.

DANNY. Just think there's a, a time and a –

VIV. The time is now. No point getting all your qualifications and that, bits of paper then standing there like a fucking, ornament. Garden gnome. You're an athlete, Danny. Behave like one.

DANNY. I did say I was shit in goal.

VIV. Not that shit.

Right. Beardy.

GEOFF. Here we go.

VIV. The fuck is that on your head?

GEOFF. It's a hat, Viv.

VIV. Don't think it belongs on a football pitch really, do you?

GEOFF. My lucky hat.

VIV. Not that lucky.

GEOFF. I did score.

VIV. For the wrong team.

GEOFF. Alright, no need to. I just. My sort of, isn't it? My thing.

VIV. Rest of us manage without a thing.

GEOFF. Rest of us manage without a bra, Viv. Not saying you should.

VIV. My bra's not dangerous. That –

GEOFF. It's wool.

VIV. Saw them, Geoff. Saw them yanking your tassels.

GEOFF. Only flirting.

VIV. Not flirting that's bloody, garotting.

GEOFF. Don't see why you're so fussed.

VIV. Cos it looks like you're not taking it seriously. The team.

GEOFF. I'm not taking it seriously.

JOE. Geoff.

GEOFF. Well, I'm not. Meant to be a laugh isn't it? I thought? Sort of, comedy team names, nothing too, just, banter, jumpers for, for goalposts. Six weeks, four teams, play each other twice. Sunday afternoon fun. Suddenly we're on this proper pitch you're all… No shame in losing to the lesbians, Viv. They're really good. Probably win the league. Won't make a scrap of difference, this. And anyway, always wear it. Bath. In bed. Work. Tell her, Joe.

LUKE. Where d'you work, Geoff?

GEOFF. Oh. D'you know Marks and Spencer's?

LUKE *nods*.

Just in the doorway. Of Marks and Spencer's.

DANNY. Geoff's a busker.

VIV. He's a twat.

GEOFF. At the moment, busker. Eventually though, I'm thinking: gay icon. Long as I've got this.

VIV *huffs*.

Look if you really want to bring everyone down, get all heavy and that, whatever – covers my scar up. Sick of everyone going on about it. (*To* LUKE.) I got gay-bashed. Got a scar. Thought: keep this on. Till I'm mended.

LUKE. Sorry, Geoff.

GEOFF. Nah it's. Don't let it get me down. If anything it's spurred me on, career-wise.

VIV. Where next – a bigger doorway?

GEOFF. The main stage. At Hull Pride.

VIV. What you on about?

GEOFF. They're auditioning people, sort of *X Factor*-y, for Hull Pride. You just, you sing a song, whoever's best gets a slot, main stage, in front of, you know: everyone. Everyone in Hull. Reckon, I can win that, suddenly I'm getting, the bookings are flooding in – pubs, weddings, care homes, the lot. Just need to find the right song. Also: keep my hat on. So it's not negotiable.

Was there anything else football-wise?

VIV *sighs*.

VIV. Maybe just, try and score for us next week.

GEOFF. Do my best.

JOE. What about you, Viv?

VIV. I'll try an' all.

JOE. No I mean, your notes?

VIV (*reads*). 'Bollock everyone.'

Job done.

DANNY. We're really not that bad.

VIV. Wouldn't've even had a team if Luke hadn't turned up.

GEOFF. Yeah cheers, Luke.

JOE. Nice one.

LUKE. No it was, Danny brought the poster in, to the library.

VIV. What you on about, poster?

GEOFF (*smiling*). Yeah, Danny. Tell us more about this poster.

DANNY. Just did some posters. For the team.

GEOFF. How many posters?

DANNY. Geoff, shut up.

VIV. News to me.

DANNY. Thought: recruitment drive.

LUKE. And I was, I work there, Danny said could he put this poster up on the, we've got like this noticeboard, for the community, the community noticeboard. And I said yeah. Saw what it was for, just thought: go for it.

VIV. Well, thank fuck you did, love. Frankly. Didn't see that much evidence of you going for it but –

JOE. Viv.

LUKE. No it's, I get it. Could do better.

VIV. The thing you need to remember, all of you: you're out there, we're out there, representing my pub, alright? My pub. Wanted to do two things last year: one: carry the Olympic torch through the streets of Hull; two: win Pub of the Year. Did I manage either? Did I fuck. Not asking for much this year but I don't think winning a few football matches is beyond us.

JOE. Five weeks to go, Viv. It's not over yet.

VIV. I bought the fucking trophy.

> VIV *gets the trophy out of a carrier bag, sticks it a bit too close to* JOE's *face.*

JOE. Spot on.

VIV. We can win this league you know. We can. Worth taking it a bit more seriously.

> Cos titting about with your mates is all well and good right, but, you know, treat it with a bit more respect, treat yourselves and, you know, the team, the thought of a team, football, think about it, treat it with a bit more respect and it'll, I'm not kidding, it will enrich your lives in ways you can't even begin to imagine. It just. It just will.

> Ask the lesbians.

> *A moment.*

> Right I'm done. Pub.

GEOFF. Wahey.

> (*To* LUKE.) Pub?

> LUKE *shakes his head.*

LUKE. Better not.

GEOFF. Come on, Luke.

DANNY. One drink.

LUKE. Can't really.

VIV. It's a pub football team, Luke. Pub is half the activity.

GEOFF. At least half.

LUKE. My dad's doing Sunday dinner so. For tea. Yorkshire puddings and that. Not to be missed. And the buses are, Sundays, nightmare but –

VIV. Something wrong with my pub?

LUKE. No, course not, sounds. Lovely just. I dunno. Not really in it for the, the pub bit.

VIV. Well, you're hardly in it for the football are you?

LUKE. I am sorry.

DANNY. Viv.

VIV. Only messing aren't I?

LUKE. No but I mean. Just so you know: I do, I realise I'm. I know I'm shit. Honestly. Stood there today like, everything happening round me thinking sort of: what are you playing at, Luke? You div. Even before I got here I just, got myself into a right… Basically, what it is: forgot about throw-ins. I just, I forgot they existed. Completely. Started worrying: what happens round the edges? But then I'd already set off so. Already on the bus so, just thought: no harm really, is there, in being…? Somewhere to come from. And I've had, I've really enjoyed, had a, had a lovely afternoon so. Thanks for, yeah for, for having me and that, letting me play and. I mean I know we didn't exactly, you know but, I really just. Cheers for…

Anyway. Best be off.

He goes to the door.

JOE. See you next week, Luke.

VIV. See you, love.

GEOFF. Played, Luke.

DANNY. See you.

> LUKE *tries to leave. Pushes on the pull door. Tries again. Leaves.*

GEOFF. Thought he did alright.

VIV. Bit rabbit-in-headlights but. Give him a few weeks, reckon he'll –

DANNY. He won't come back now.

GEOFF. What you on about?

VIV. He better do. All we've got.

GEOFF. Course he'll come back.

DANNY. Doubt it.

JOE. Why wouldn't he come back?

DANNY. Cos Viv's bloody, scared him off.

> VIV *laughs.*

VIV. Good one, Danny.

DANNY. He's really shy.

VIV. So?

DANNY. So you took the piss out of him.

VIV. Shy people love it when you take the piss out of them.

GEOFF. That is true actually.

JOE. He'll come back, Danny, don't worry. Be fine.

> DANNY *huffs.*
>
> *Picks up his boots.*

DANNY. Off to clean these.

VIV. Oh do mine, love, will you?

DANNY *sighs and takes* VIV*'s boots.*

DANNY. Anyone else?

JOE. Cheers, Danny.

GEOFF *is about to pass* DANNY *his boots then realises he's annoyed.*

GEOFF. I'll do mine.

DANNY *and* GEOFF *leave with everyone's boots.*

JOE *starts to get changed.* VIV *watches him.*

VIV. Not having a shower then?

JOE. Have one at home.

VIV. What?

JOE. Be fine till I get home.

VIV. Coming for a drink though?

JOE. Not tonight.

VIV. Fuck that.

JOE. I'm knackered, Viv.

VIV. I'm knackered, I'm pushing through.

JOE. Luke's gone home. You let him.

VIV. Luke's dad has made Yorkshire puddings.

Come to the pub.

JOE. Nah.

VIV. Don't be a knob, Joe. Come.

JOE. I'm just. I've had enough.

A moment.

VIV (*in a mood*). Fine.

JOE. What?

VIV. Nothing. You're in a strop aren't you? You're in a strop cos I happened to mention that you need to work on your fitness. Which you do.

JOE. I'm off.

VIV. You're only half-dressed.

JOE. I don't care, Viv.

VIV. Always better to tackle these things head-on.

JOE *sighs*.

Nearly forty, Joe. Couple of weeks you'll be forty. Need to start looking after yourself a bit.

JOE. I am.

VIV. You're not, Joe. Well, you're not.

JOE. Don't start this now.

VIV. Not starting anything, I'm just.

Think: I'm lucky. Got Lisa to keep an eye on me. Go home she's there, isn't she? In her jeggings. Probably put the heating on, rustled up a stroganoff. You spend the whole day mending boilers, go home it's, nothing. Pot Noodle and a misery wank.

JOE. Usually just have toast.

VIV. Beardy in the spare room, cluttering up your futon.

JOE. I like Beardy staying. We're mates.

VIV. Has he paid you any rent yet? Anything?

He's taking the piss.

JOE. What am I meant to do, Viv – chuck him out? Send him back to that shitty flat so he can get kicked in again? Is that what you're saying?

VIV. I'm not here to tell you what to do, Joe.

JOE *smiles*.

Just saying: can't keep living in the past.

JOE. It's normal this, Viv. It is. This is normal.

A moment.

VIV. Let's do a cool-down. Stretches.

Come on.

JOE. Viv, I can't be arsed.

VIV. Don't stretch you'll get injuries.

JOE. Good. If it gets me out of this.

VIV *smiles and stretches.*

VIV. Lunge with me, Joe. Come on. Lunge with me.

JOE *gets up. They do some stretching.* VIV *'s quite bendy.* JOE *isn't.*

He winces a bit.

What's up?

JOE. Nothing just. Groin.

VIV. Your groin's not nothing, Joe, your groin's vital.

JOE. It'll be right.

It isn't.

VIV. D'you want me to pull your leg?

JOE. What d'you mean?

VIV. Sometimes it helps. Pulling your leg.

JOE. I can't tell if you're joking.

VIV. Course I'm not joking. Lie down.

JOE *lies down.* VIV *pulls his leg.*

JOE. Bloody hell.

VIV. See?

JOE. It's worse.

VIV. You'll feel the benefit. In a minute. You will.

Now. Shall I pull the other one?

JOE *sits up*.

What?

JOE. It does sound like you're taking the piss, Viv.

VIV. Give it here.

VIV *pulls* JOE's *other leg. He sighs*.

Better?

JOE *shakes his head*.

Well, you wouldn't be in this state if you came jogging with me.

Will you come? This week?

JOE. Maybe.

VIV. Will you though?

JOE. Maybe.

VIV. It'll help. It will.

No answer.

D'you know why I'm doing this, Joe? The team?

JOE. Cos the lesbians said you were bossy.

VIV (*smiling*). Fuck off.

Cos I'm worried about you.

JOE. Viv.

VIV. Every Sunday, Joe. Every Sunday.

JOE. What you on about?

VIV. You know what I'm on about.

JOE *looks down*.

Thought of you just standing there, all afternoon. By yourself.

JOE. Come with me then.

Just be there. Where she is. Just for a minute.

VIV. We're better here, Joe. We are. I know it's… You've lost your wife, I've lost my big sister. And you miss her. I know. I miss her. It's hard, and. And this is the last place your average thirty-nine-year-old straight man wants to be on a Sunday afternoon but. Better than… It is.

JOE. I got her a bunch of flowers every Sunday, Viv. From when we first started going out. Just what I did. For nineteen years. Doesn't feel right stopping now.

VIV. Humour me, Joe, just. Humour me.

A moment.

JOE *smiles.*

JOE. Maybe.

GEOFF *and* DANNY *come back in.* DANNY *gives them their boots back.*

All done?

DANNY *nods.*

GEOFF. Yep, just talking about how Danny fancies Luke.

DANNY. We weren't.

GEOFF. You do though.

DANNY. Fuck off.

GEOFF. What was all that poster stuff then?

DANNY. Put a poster up. For the team.

GEOFF. One poster. In the library. Which you only started going to cos of Luke.

DANNY. Cos of my course.

GEOFF. That's why he was playing shit today. Distracted by Luke.

DANNY. Just thought this, the, the team might be up his street.

VIV. He's up your street.

DANNY. Viv.

GEOFF. Made him a poster, Danny.

DANNY. For the team.

GEOFF. Used glitter glue.

DANNY. You haven't seen – the other posters on that noticeboard, Zumba, the Freedom Chorus, properly snazzy.

VIV. Just ask him out, love. Much less faff.

GEOFF. That's what I said.

DANNY. I can't.

GEOFF. Why not?

DANNY. You know why not, Geoff.

GEOFF. Got his number haven't you?

    DANNY *nods*.

VIV. Well then, don't see what's –

DANNY. No, you don't, cos it's none of your business so just. Leave it.

VIV. Very mysterious, Danny.

DANNY. Don't need this alright? Leave it be.

    A moment.

JOE. Shall us lot head to the pub?

VIV. Oh you're coming now are you?

JOE. Someone has to get Beardy's drinks.

GEOFF. Piss up!

VIV. Or, make a plan to beat the shit out of Man City next week.

JOE. Either's fine. Catch us up, Danny, when you're…?

They leave.

A moment.

DANNY *looks at his phone.*

GEOFF*'s head pops up at a window.*

GEOFF (*spooky voice*). Ring Luke, Danny.

Without turning round, DANNY *sticks two fingers up at* GEOFF. GEOFF *disappears.*

DANNY *gets a brush. Sweeps.*

Looks at his phone. Deep breath.

DANNY *rings* LUKE.

LUKE*'s bag starts ringing. It's under one of the benches. He's forgotten it.*

DANNY. Shit.

He picks up LUKE*'s bag.*

Fuck.

DANNY *stops the call. Looks at* LUKE*'s bag for a bit.*

LUKE *comes back in.*

LUKE. Oh, you've got it, cheers.

Saw Viv and that, said you were still…

DANNY. You alright?

LUKE. Yeah. What a knob.

DANNY *smiles.*

Got on the bus, couldn't find my ticket. And normally I'd just get a new one but I couldn't, no money cos, lost my wallet an' all. Thought don't panic, just get off, ring Danny, see if I'd left it here but then, no phone either. I was like: how can I lose all my stuff on the same day? How is that even possible? Then I remembered: bag.

DANNY. Got everything now?

> LUKE *shows* DANNY.

LUKE. Ticket. Wallet. Phone. Um.

DANNY. What's that?

LUKE. Oh nothing just. You know.

> LUKE *holds up a tatty notebook. It's covered in stuff and says 'DIARY' on the front.*

DANNY. Diary diary?

> LUKE *nods.*

LUKE. Yeah I know it's a bit. I mean my life is sort of really boring but then for some reason I feel the need to record it in quite a lot of detail.

In case I forget, I think.

That it's boring.

DANNY. Bet it's not boring.

LUKE. It really is.

DANNY. Prove it.

> LUKE *finds a good page, reads:*

LUKE. Thursday:

'Porridge boiled over in the microwave this morning. It is actually quite a tricky stain to clean so I missed the 77. Got the 75 instead. It goes via Burstwick and Holderness Road. Got in late. Spent two hours trying to reshelve Mills and Boons without disturbing a sleeping tramp. Jacket potato for lunch.'

DANNY. That's who you remind me of: Bridget Jones.

> LUKE *nods.*

LUKE. Except gay. And from Patrington. And a tit.

> DANNY *smiles.* LUKE *notices his phone.*

Did you ring me?

DANNY. What's up?

LUKE. Missed call. From you.

DANNY. Oh yeah just. Yeah.

Letting you know. About your bag and that.

LUKE. D'you want a hand clearing up? Probably do it wrong
but.

DANNY. You're alright.

LUKE. I mean I'll have a go.

DANNY. Nah, it's technically my job so.

Karen lets us have it for free, the pitch and that, long as I
clear up. My boss.

LUKE. You work here?

DANNY. Well, I just. I help with some of the youth teams and
that, holiday activities, coaching but it's not. It's my
placement. For my course.

LUKE. Sounds fun.

DANNY. Yeah it's, yeah.

Not going that well to be honest. My course. Get all these
assignments and, I'm just, I'm shit. Just want to do the
coaching bits. But then, struggle a bit with that an' all. Cos
the others are all dead cocky sort of. That's why, one of the
reasons why. Thought I could practise on you lot but. Wasn't
quite ready for Viv.

LUKE. She seems quite passionate about football.

DANNY. No stopping her.

A moment.

LUKE. Better go. Again.

LUKE *heads off again.*

DANNY. See you next week then?

LUKE. Course, yeah.

LUKE *struggles with the door.*

DANNY. It's a pull, Luke.

LUKE. Sorry?

DANNY. Um. Pull?

DANNY *pulls the door.*

LUKE *looks embarrassed and leaves.*

Week Two

VOICE ON RADIO. Lesbian Rovers, 4 – Tranny United, 2, Man City, 7 – Barely Athletic, 0.

JOE, LUKE, GEOFF and DANNY look a bit tense. JOE is particularly sweaty. VIV enters from the showers with her shower cap and towel.

VIV. Right, think the thing to do, the best thing to do is just: pretend that, that match, that match we just lost seven-nil… pretend that never happened. Alright just, let's just draw a line. Start looking forwards.

VIV sits down. She gets a book out of her bag. Looks at it. Everyone is a bit surprised.

JOE. What's this, Viv?

VIV holds the book up.

VIV. Luke found me it. Library.

JOE reads.

JOE. *Coaching Junior Football Teams. For Dummies.*

DANNY. You're coaching us now?

VIV. Thought I'd try.

GEOFF. Bit harsh isn't it? The, the –

VIV. I said that. As if I'm a dummy.

GEOFF. I was thinking more –

VIV. I know exactly what you were thinking, Beardy. But if you honestly believe sitting there in your little hat you deserve to be treated as anything other than a junior football team you've got another thing coming. Shame they didn't have one for toddlers.

DANNY. Viv's back.

VIV. No I didn't… Just a sec.

> VIV *takes a deep breath*.

> Realised last week with you all I made a, I made a mistake. I
> was frustrated cos I didn't think you were all, I know you
> can all. Hang on.

> *She checks the book.*

> What I want to do: I want to share with you my 'coaching
> philosophy'. Which I should've done before we started
> apparently but I didn't have the book then. Anyway,
> coaching philosophy, here it is:

> Do. Your. Best.

> Do your best.

> *A moment.*

DANNY. Brilliant.

VIV. Thing is: I've worked it out what upsets me, it's not the
losing it's, well, it is the losing obviously but, it's not the, not
the fact we've lost a match –

GEOFF. Two matches.

VIV. It's not that it's, it is the fact that we haven't done our best.
I am someone who likes to see people doing their best. And I
expect, that is what I expect of you. So just. Yeah. Do your
best. Cos I know you all, well, don't know Luke that well
but, the rest of you, known you for years haven't I? Know
what you're all capable of, what you can do if you just. So
let's just. The past two matches, put them behind us. Fresh
start. And we'll… I'm not asking you to win. I'm asking you
to just: chuck your face at it, have a, have a fucking good go
at it. And then we'll. Yeah. We'll see.

GEOFF. Yeah.

VIV. Good.

LUKE. Really good yeah.

JOE. Well said.

VIV. I'm glad. Good.

A moment.

DANNY. Not much coaching was there?

VIV. I've only read Chapter One, Danny. Skipped most of it.

Anyway, that's your job.

DANNY. Oh.

VIV. Thing is: I'm more about inspiring people. Vision and that. Thought you could do the nuts and bolts. Cos it's one thing standing there in goal watching me make clanger after clanger isn't it? Thinking you could do better. Very easy to do that but. You could just do better. Be a bit, proactive.

DANNY. Sorry, Viv.

VIV. Don't be sorry, be proactive.

Well, go on then.

DANNY. Go on what?

VIV. What d'you suggest? If you were sorting us out, what would you do?

DANNY. I haven't really –

VIV. Danny, this is boring, come on.

DANNY. Fine.

DANNY *thinks.*

Spose: Joe?

Viv mentioned before, you're not the fittest.

JOE. She did.

DANNY. Looked a bit hot and bothered today. And you have been limping since that jog.

JOE *nods.*

Wonder if we should try you in goal maybe? Thing is: it's mainly standing still. That alright?

JOE. Love a good stand. I sometimes think in another life I might've been a bollard.

DANNY. Wicked.

And then. Well. Luke.

LUKE *smiles*.

First things first – cheers for coming back.

LUKE. Cheers for having me.

DANNY. The main thing I'd say to you is: don't be too cautious. Like, thing is: you make a lot of chances for other people, Beardy and Viv especially, but sometimes you'll pass to them rather than have a shot yourself. And I know you're not, you're not that confident yet but, nothing bad'll happen. Promise. We're all missing, cocking up. But if you don't have a go you definitely won't score. And I think you might be alright if you let yourself so. Just, yeah. Have a go.

LUKE. Do my best.

DANNY. Mega. Viv.

VIV. Assistant Coach Danny.

DANNY *smiles*.

DANNY. Think it's great you're keeping an eye on what everyone else is doing, chatting and, and feedback and that. Tips. That is really helpful.

GEOFF. Really helpful.

VIV. But…

DANNY. But then some of your play's a bit… Well, I dunno. Reckon you could maybe do to take more time with some of your choices. Think you tend to just, see the ball coming towards you, fucking: boot it. Which is great but. Lot of volleys today. Thing is: the goal's only this high. Keep it low, controlled, got a bit more chance of going in.

VIV. Fair enough.

DANNY. And then, I dunno, maybe also worth doing the same thing with, yeah. Advice? Sort of, deep breath before you…

VIV *looks annoyed, then takes a deep breath.*

VIV. I hear you.

DANNY *is surprised.*

DANNY. Okay then. Right. Beardy?

GEOFF *holds his hat.*

GEOFF. The hat is staying.

DANNY. Not the hat that's the problem.

GEOFF. Good.

What is the problem?

DANNY. Well, it's a bit… Felt like there was quite a lot of aggression out there, I thought, today, in the tackling.

GEOFF. Yeah, cheers for the back-up, guys.

DANNY. Not their fault.

GEOFF. You especially. Meant to be my wingman.

DANNY. I was in goal.

Anyway, point is: d'you think there's a reason why they might've been picking on you like that? Specifically Sean?

VIV. Which one's Sean?

DANNY. Captain. Angry-looking.

GEOFF. Leave it, Danny.

VIV. What's going on?

DANNY. Wondered if maybe there's a bit of baggage there?

GEOFF. Oh that's right, have a go at me. Just cos I had some sex.

VIV. You've shagged the opposition?

GEOFF. Yeah. And it didn't go that well if I'm honest so just. Don't sort of…

VIV. When was this?

GEOFF. Friday night. Just, few drinks and that. Bit of a dance. Everyone's off home so thought: back to his cos. Sean's cos, he's all, you know. Buff. Got this new flat on the marina, properly nice, lights across the Humber and that, twinkling. Pours us a drink. Dims the dimmer switch. And I can tell it's heading, yeah, cos: puts some music on, puts his iTunes on, the playlist's called: 'Lovemaking'. Then, middle of, he's just sucking me off, d'you know what comes on? On his iTunes? Bloody, Enya.

VIV. So?

JOE (*amused*). So he left.

VIV. You left?

GEOFF. Course I left. Course I did.

I was like: 'I can't do this, Sean. I just can't do this to "Orinoco Flow".'

But then now there's like this weird tension or something so…

VIV. Right. You: no more sex.

GEOFF. Yeah good one.

VIV. I mean it. No more sexing of the opposition. Pre-match ban. Starting now.

GEOFF. Thing is, Viv: them lads, Man City, they are my main reason for doing this so –

VIV. Keep it in your pants, keep it off the pitch.

GEOFF *isn't convinced*.

Get as much action as you like once we've won. Victory sex. Imagine. But till that trophy's in my pub… It's for your own good, Beardy.

A moment.

GEOFF. Fine.

> *Points at his groin.*

> No more fun. You hear?

VIV. That's us done then, I reckon. See how it goes next week. I've got to swap with Lisa now. Pub?

LUKE. Bus.

> LUKE *gets his stuff, tries to leave. Pushes on the pull door.*

> Every time.

> *Leaves.*

JOE. I'll come with you, Viv.

VIV. You need a shower first.

JOE. Be fine.

VIV. No, catch me up, Joe. I just got a waft.

> JOE *gets his towel and some shower gel, goes for a shower.*

GEOFF. I'm helping Danny.

DANNY. I have actually asked you not to help.

GEOFF. Not help help, just take the piss.

VIV. In a bit then.

> VIV *leaves.* DANNY *gets the sweeping brush.* GEOFF *is grinning.*

DANNY. Don't.

GEOFF. What?

DANNY. Don't want to talk about it.

GEOFF. Really?

> GEOFF *gets his guitar. It has been through the wars a bit, and is painted pink.*

> Play you my song then. Potential song. For Pride. And just, let me know initial thoughts.

DANNY. Okay.

DANNY is sweeping.

GEOFF. Well, you have to listen though.

DANNY. I can listen and sweep.

GEOFF. I need your undivided attention.

Come on, Danny. Only got a month.

DANNY. A month. To think of one song.

GEOFF. Knew you wouldn't understand. It's cos you've never busked.

DANNY smiles.

You laugh but. Want to do it properly, got to ask yourself, you know: the big questions. Both of them. One: what is the song these people, in front of me, not connected, what is the song that will make their day better? Reach out, grab them, lift them up a bit. And that's only… Two: the toughie. Got to look inside yourself, properly look inside, ask yourself this: if my heart had a voice, what would it sing? Otherwise you're not a busker are you? Just a knob in a hat. And there's maybe one song, in the world, that is the answer to both those questions. That's what I'm looking for. Got to find that song.

DANNY. You're overthinking this.

Reckon just: pick something gay. Uplifting.

GEOFF. Well. See what you think. This is just: first attempt.

But, just so you know, not just singing this for me. Singing it for, for anyone who needs to hear it. Dedicated to, yeah. To a fairer world.

A breath.

GEOFF *sings 'Please, Please, Please, Let Me Get What I Want' by The Smiths.*

A moment.

DANNY. How's that gay and uplifting?

GEOFF. Don't know anything gay and uplifting do I?

DANNY. You know Wham!.

GEOFF. Too naff.

DANNY. It is for Pride, Beardy.

GEOFF. Why is that naff though? Should be, important should be…

GEOFF *lifts his hat up. He's got a big scar on his head.*

Look at this. Is it naff? No. It's rugged. But it's also, you know. Not there yet, are we? Feel like a bit of a dickhead standing up singing how everything's great and that when like there's people still thinking it's okay, fair enough to hang around outside my flat, drag me into an alley, kick the shit out of me. For a laugh.

No. Doing this, doing it properly.

A moment.

Not spot-on though, The Smiths. Lol.

GEOFF *puts his guitar down.*

Sure you're alright?

DANNY. Yeah, course.

GEOFF. Just, I know you said you don't want to talk about it but then I think, secretly, you do want to talk about it.

DANNY. I don't want to talk about it.

GEOFF. Okay.

He starts sweeping again.

DANNY. Cos, thing is, it's just… It's not a good plan.

GEOFF. How come?

DANNY. You know how come. Anyway, anyway I don't –

GEOFF. I know why you think it's not a good plan, that doesn't mean it's not a good plan.

DANNY. Well, it isn't so –

GEOFF. Why though?

DANNY. Beardy, don't.

GEOFF. Don't what?

DANNY. Be a dick.

GEOFF. I'm being a dick? You're the one –

DANNY. What?

GEOFF. Crawled across two years of fucking, wilderness, the wilderness years, nothing, finally found someone you like, who is decent, actually, who likes you, won't do anything about it. I'm just saying: why not?

DANNY. You know why.

GEOFF *sighs*.

What?

GEOFF. Nothing just: if that's your reason, not going anywhere is it?

DANNY. I realise that.

GEOFF. And, yeah, it is a reason to be sort of. Careful. But it's not a reason to never ever do anything again. Cos, thing is: you do everything right. You do. There's loads of people, Danny, who manage to, like you would be. More than manage. If you didn't know about it, would you have asked him out?

DANNY *nods*.

So ask him. Start something. Cos otherwise we'll still be sitting here, Danny – we will – old men. Flat caps, bladder issues, you still going 'not a good plan, not yet'.

DANNY. Thing is: if I tell him, and it goes wrong, that's like, the first time I've told someone, and the first time it's gone wrong. That's a hundred per cent wrong. And I just, I think it is quite important for me to feel like things are not a hundred per cent wrong.

GEOFF. No way are things a hundred per cent wrong.

Explain things, give him the chance, he'll get it. But you have to give him chance. And then it's done and you can just, be careful. See how you get on. Just be two people being careful. Seeing how they get on.

Open the love gates, Danny. Let it pour out.

A moment.

DANNY. You think, definitely, he likes me?

GEOFF *nods*.

GEOFF. I sense Viv's right. He's not here for the football.

DANNY. What now then?

GEOFF *shrugs, goes in for a joke snog*.

GEOFF. I've always been a fan of the drunken lunge.

DANNY *avoids it*.

DANNY. Brilliant.

GEOFF. Have a proper chat to him, Danny. Explain it. So he knows there's a risk but also, he knows how small it is. Long as you're careful, keep an eye on things, use protection. Probably work out amazing, Danny. It will. Probably work out, really good.

DANNY *looks doubtful*.

JOE *comes back in*.

Someone smells nice.

JOE *holds up his shower gel*.

JOE (*quietly*). Ylang-ylang.

GEOFF. Very manly.

JOE. On offer in Tesco's. Different types. I had to decide if I'd rather have a silky glow or be deeply nourished. Went for the glow. Not sure it's worked. Can I have a word, Danny?

DANNY. Course.

JOE. Been thinking in the shower. Thing is: I'm not goalie material. At all.

DANNY. Don't be daft.

JOE. Seriously, I'm not a hundred per cent sure I can catch. Got enough on my plate without being the only reason we lose to Tranny bloody United.

GEOFF. Doubt you'll be the only reason, Joe.

JOE. Still though.

DANNY. You'll be fine.

JOE. And it's my birthday. Next week.

GEOFF. Fuck's sake, Danny. 'You'll be fine.' That the best you can do?

GEOFF *gets one end of the middle bench.*

Grab this.

DANNY *helps* GEOFF *move the bench back against the wall.*

JOE. What's happening?

GEOFF. That's the goal, right. You're the keeper.

JOE. Oh, Beardy, no.

GEOFF. Yes. Yes. And me and Danny, we'll just kick the odd ball at you, nothing to be scared of. You just stand there, spread your arms out, think wide thoughts.

JOE. Honestly I –

GEOFF *kicks a ball.*

DANNY. Fucking hell, Geoff.

GEOFF. Sorry, bit hard.

DANNY. Mind the –

GEOFF. What? What can I possibly make any shitter in here?

DANNY. Windows?

GEOFF. Eyes on the ball, Joe. Eyes on the ball.

DANNY *kicks it very gently.* JOE *stops it easily.*

Don't patronise him, Danny.

JOE *laughs.*

No, Joe, he is, he's patronising you. Do it properly. Kick it properly.

DANNY. Think maybe it's better to build up slowly. Confidence-wise.

GEOFF. Kick the bastard!

DANNY. I will kick it but –

GEOFF. Kick it!

DANNY. Fine.

DANNY *kicks it a bit harder.* JOE *misses again.*

JOE. Sorry.

DANNY. Joe, it's fine.

GEOFF. My go!

GEOFF *boots it.* JOE *misses.*

JOE. No chance.

DANNY *hesitates.*

GEOFF. Go on then.

DANNY. I just think if we like, leave marks or something –

GEOFF. Don't be a knob, Danny.

DANNY. If I piss Karen off I mess up my whole placement.

GEOFF. This is good coaching, she'd love it. Go.

DANNY *kicks it through* JOE*'s legs*.

Right it's not working, shit idea, soz. Plan B.

JOE. Come on then.

GEOFF. One: we set up a little goal in the garden, Joe, practise every night, in an ideal world you will just get better, somehow, dunno how. Two: have a post-match birthday celebration so whatever happens Viv can't be too angry with us, especially Joe, cos it's his birthday. Three: engineer an early getaway for you, me and Viv, Danny gives Luke a friendly lift home, save him running off to the bus. Next stop, wooing. Foolproof. What d'you reckon?

DANNY *looks doubtful*. JOE *smiles*.

JOE. That is a sort of genius, Beardy.

GEOFF *chucks* DANNY *his phone*.

GEOFF. Ring Luke. Tell him to fetch a cake.

Week Three

VOICE ON RADIO. Lesbian Rovers, 2 – Man City, 2. Tranny
United, 1 – Barely Athletic, 4.

The room is decorated for JOE's *birthday celebrations.
Balloons. There's a banner on the back wall, it says 'HAPPY
BIRTHDAY JOE!' in big, friendly letters. Another says 'YOU
OLD GIT'. There's a cake with candles. Everyone's drinking
cans of Guinness, apart from* DANNY, *who's got a Capri-
Sun .*

JOE *blows out his candles. Everyone cheers.*

VIV. At. Fucking. Last. This is it, lads. New leaf.

JOE. Maybe.

VIV. What you on about 'maybe'? Spot-on today. All of you.
Focused, committed, brilliant.

JOE. I'm not sure this lot were taking it as seriously as the other
teams.

DANNY. D'you think?

JOE. I was expecting skirts. I wasn't expecting heels.

LUKE. Did you see them at half-time? All that vodka?

GEOFF. Thought it was water.

LUKE. Oh maybe. Do Smirnoff make water?

VIV. A win is a win, lads. That's the thing to focus on. They had
a good time, we got the result we were after. And Man City
drew with the lesbians so, closing the gap. Don't think it'd
be going too far to say: this is a significant moment in the
history of Barely Athletic. Four goals. Two for assistant
coach Danny –

GEOFF. You should be moonwalking, assistant coach Danny.

VIV. Two for head coach Viv.

GEOFF. And you.

VIV. First three points. It's all, it's plain sailing from hereon in. Probably a good time to…

VIV hands JOE *a present.*

Happy birthday, love. From Danny too, we went halves.

JOE. You didn't have to.

DANNY. Open it.

JOE *does. It's a goalkeeper shirt. It says 'TOKEN STRAIGHT' on the back.*

JOE. Oh this is. Cheers.

DANNY. Thought it'd stop everyone hitting on you.

JOE. Very thoughtful. Thank you.

VIV. Group prezzie actually.

DANNY *and* VIV *unveil their new shirts.* DANNY*'s says 'ASSISTANT COACH DANNY' on the back.* VIV*'s says 'HEAD COACH VIV'.* DANNY *passes one to* LUKE *and* GEOFF *too.*

Help us look a bit more, teamy. Teamier.

GEOFF *takes his top off. And his hat.*

Quick, Luke.

LUKE. What's up?

VIV. Grab the bastard.

LUKE. I don't –

VIV. His hat.

VIV *lunges for* GEOFF*'s hat.* GEOFF *picks it up and pops it back on. Beams. His shirt says 'BEARDY' on the back.*

GEOFF. I look and feel like a champion.

LUKE *is looking at his top. He is wide-eyed.*

VIV. Alright, Luke?

LUKE. Seen this?

He shows the others. It says 'BRIDGET' on the back. He's delighted.

And I will, I'll write about it, in my diary. So it's sort of… Thank you, Viv.

LUKE *hugs* VIV. *She's generally not a huggy person.*

VIV. Oh. From Danny an' all.

LUKE. Course. Cheers, Danny.

LUKE *doesn't know whether to hug* DANNY *or not.*

DANNY. Pleasure, mate.

DANNY *sort of gently punches* LUKE.

GEOFF. Mate?

JOE. Put it on then.

LUKE *puts it on top of his other top.*

VIV. Oh get it on properly, love, you'll roast like that.

LUKE. I'm fine.

GEOFF. Good plan. Danny might perv.

DANNY. What?

GEOFF. Is it about time we were heading off? Joe?

VIV. Not even started the cake. Luke's made this.

JOE. You didn't, Luke?

LUKE. No I didn't actually. It was my mum. I just did the stirring. Most of the stirring.

JOE. Oh cheers. And say, to your mum –

GEOFF. Take a bit with us maybe? Joe?

JOE. Good plan.

VIV. No rush is there.

GEOFF. There is a rush. There bloody is.

VIV. What you on about?

GEOFF. It's tagine o'clock, Viv. Got to get back to ours. For the tagine.

VIV. If I hear one more word about this fucking tagine.

LUKE. What tagine?

VIV. Don't ask.

GEOFF. Got this tagine. The pot thing. With a chimney. I say got, found. In a skip. But it is like: phenomenal. So me, Viv, Lisa, Joe, we're having a night of delicious slow-cooked Moroccan flavours to celebrate Joe's new-found middle-age. I've been gathering ingredients all week.

VIV. Nicking them. Off me.

GEOFF. Be worth it, Viv, I promise. I would've asked you, Luke, but thought you'd need to get back to your dad's Yorkshire puddings, and Danny's got his assignment to do. But anyway, we need to go. Wagons roll.

VIV. Lisa's at the pub for another hour.

GEOFF. Yeah but –

VIV. Might as well stay here. Celebrate our first win. As a team.

GEOFF. That would be nice but I need to stir my tagine.

VIV. Be fine, Beardy.

GEOFF. Two words: chickpeas.

VIV. The longer you leave them, the better they are. More tender.

GEOFF. Oh for once will you just –

VIV. What?

GEOFF. I dunno. Fucking, cooperate.

Danny's got to clear up here, lock up, drop Luke home, finish his assignment. I've got to drain my pulses.

VIV. Well, it's Joe's birthday and Joe's happy here.

And that's. Isn't it? First time I've seen him happy for, months.

GEOFF. First time you're not having a go at him for months.

JOE. Beardy.

GEOFF. Well, it's true.

VIV. Fuck off it is. When have I had a go at you, Joe?

JOE. Let's not do this now.

VIV. I keep an eye on you, look out for you. You're my brother-in-law. Don't have a go at you.

GEOFF. Doesn't need anyone keeping an eye on him.

VIV. Course he doesn't, he's got you staying at his house, for free, getting tagines out of skips.

JOE. Viv.

VIV. Sorry just. Sick of everyone going on, about all… And I do actually, I worry about you.

JOE. No need to worry tonight.

VIV. I do though.

DANNY. Viv.

VIV. I do. And I don't really… Thought: get you out of the house a bit. Good start. Take your mind off… That's wrong, apparently. Now we're having an argument about it. On your birthday. Well done, Viv, foot in it again.

VIV's a bit upset with herself.

JOE. Well. What are you worried about?

VIV. Everything.

JOE. Can you narrow it down?

VIV. Worried you're depressed aren't I?

JOE. I'm not depressed.

VIV. Denial's part of it, Joe. I've googled it.

JOE. I'm sad, I'm not...

VIV. Just want you to be alright.

JOE. I am.

VIV. Only alright though.

JOE. Only alright's fine isn't it? For now.

   More worried about you to be honest.

VIV. What you on about me? I'm fine.

JOE. You do seem fine.

   She doesn't.

   Shall we have this tagine then?

   You two make friends.

   VIV *and* GEOFF *sulk.*

   Maybe make friends in the car. Played, lads.

   JOE *leaves.* VIV *follows.*

   GEOFF *stands up. Beams.*

GEOFF. I wish you both a brilliant night.

   He leaves.

   A moment.

LUKE. Hope they'll be alright.

DANNY. They will be. Lisa's good at sorting, stuff.

LUKE. She must be quite a good listener.

DANNY. She's, top.

   Come to the pub one night, meet her.

LUKE. Maybe. I dunno actually, I don't really. I'm not very pubby to be honest. I'm more sort of, stay-in-on-my-own-y. With a book or. Don't even drink that much normally. I mean not that, this is, yeah –

DANNY. Don't have to drink it if you don't want.

LUKE. I didn't want to waste it.

DANNY. I'll finish it.

LUKE. What about driving?

DANNY. Only half a can isn't it? Be fine.

LUKE wipes the top of the can with his sleeve.

What you doing?

LUKE. Just wiping the spit off.

He gives the can to DANNY. DANNY *is smiling.*

What?

DANNY. Nothing. Cheers.

LUKE. Why you smiling?

DANNY. Dunno, you're funny.

LUKE sighs.

What's up?

LUKE. Nothing. Just feel like I keep making a massive tit of myself, it's a bit…

DANNY. Not massive.

LUKE nods, smiles, a bit sad.

LUKE. We should, um.

DANNY. What?

LUKE. Um. Sweep?

DANNY. Oh, yeah.

LUKE. D'you want to do it yourself? The sweeping? Don't want to get it wrong.

DANNY. You won't get it wrong.

LUKE. I probably will.

DANNY. Luke.

LUKE. Honestly, I can get anything wrong. It's like a
superpower.

    DANNY *touches* LUKE *on the shoulder.* LUKE *looks up.*

DANNY. Um.

LUKE. What's…?

DANNY. Nothing just. Just wondered if. I just.

LUKE. What?

DANNY. Um. I'd really like to kiss you, Luke. If that's…

LUKE. Are you sure?

    DANNY *laughs. Nods.*

    They kiss. It's a gentle one.

    A moment. LUKE *laughs.*

DANNY. What?

LUKE. Taste of, thingy.

    DANNY *laughs.*

DANNY. Soz.

LUKE. No it's, nice.

DANNY. Oh now it's nice.

    A moment.

    You alright?

LUKE. Yeah I'm fine. Think I'm just a bit.

    LUKE *breathes out.*

    You know.

DANNY. Sure?

LUKE. We should get off. Home. We should be getting off home.

DANNY. It's alright.

LUKE. Your assignment though.

DANNY. It's fine. Are you worried?

LUKE. No just –

DANNY. Yorkshire puddings.

LUKE. No. Well, yeah but.

DANNY. We can still make it back before –

LUKE. Don't even like them to be honest. My dad's anyway. They're shit. It's cos: my mum's favourite, Yorkshire puddings. But then she cooks everything all week so my dad just sort of decided he'd do Sunday dinner but, as a gesture but, thing is, he's so shit, my mum ends up doing it all anyway. He just does the Yorkshire puddings. Badly. But then he is weirdly precious about it.

Deep breath.

Sorry this has thrown me a bit. I mean I was already, got my top and I was like: oh my God I'm actually on a team. With a nickname. That's like, appropriate. Cos it's. Not really had one before, normally just, people in the past just went for sort of, Bender, whatever. But: a snog! That is, even better. Honestly. And it's, yeah. First one, actually. I know: pathetic, like I'm all, I'm nineteen but. I'm from Patrington, work in a library it's. Slim pickings, if I'm honest. Cos, can't snog a book, can you? My mum said that. Well, she said you can but, they don't snog back. Which is actually just, you know. The truth.

DANNY. Just a little kiss, Luke.

LUKE. I know.

DANNY. You can have another.

LUKE. I'd love that.

DANNY *laughs*.

DANNY. Come here.

He pulls LUKE *towards him, kisses him. Tender. Starts to take* LUKE's *top off, gently.* LUKE *jumps, moves away. Quick.*

You alright?

LUKE. Yeah, yeah.

DANNY. What's up?

LUKE. Nothing. I dunno.

DANNY. You sure?

LUKE. Yeah.

A moment.

DANNY. Sorry.

LUKE. No.

DANNY. Got a bit –

LUKE. Yeah, no.

DANNY *smiles.*

DANNY. Worried I'll peep?

LUKE. Not much to look at.

DANNY. Probably would peep though. To be honest.

LUKE *wrinkles his nose.*

A moment.

Take it off?

LUKE *shakes his head.*

Only me.

LUKE. Exactly.

DANNY. Take mine off an' all.

LUKE. It's not that.

DANNY. Or, maybe, you could take mine off?

LUKE. Nah.

DANNY. Well, it's coming off.

DANNY *takes his top off. Smiles.*

There. Your go.

LUKE. I'm really not –

DANNY. Your go, Luke.

LUKE *takes his first top off.*

One down.

LUKE. Danny –

DANNY. I get it, you're shy, I know. And, like, you don't have to. If you don't want to. But I think maybe you want to.

DANNY *touches the bottom of* LUKE*'s second top.* LUKE *holds it down.*

LUKE. You have to promise not to take the piss.

DANNY (*gently*). Come on then.

DANNY *takes* LUKE*'s top off.*

He's got a thermal vest on underneath. Tucked into his shorts.

Fucking hell, Luke.

LUKE. Don't.

DANNY. A vest though? A real-life thermal vest.

LUKE. Thing is: I just, I feel the cold. Get really chilly so, thought, you know. Layers.

Regretting it now.

DANNY *is smiling.*

What?

DANNY. Nothing just. Think I just fell in love. A bit.

LUKE *doesn't know what to say.*

Wondering: this week if we could. If you were free one night we could maybe sort of, do, something?

LUKE. Yeah I'm, I'm free. Every night.

LUKE *looks worried.*

DANNY. Sure you're alright?

LUKE. Thing is, I'm actually. I'm a bit of a nervous gay so.

DANNY. No?

LUKE. So if we could just sort of go, steady that'd be. Slow even, that'd be…

DANNY. Taken us three months to manage a snog, Luke, think we've set quite a good pace.

A moment.

LUKE *smiles.*

LUKE. Two snogs.

DANNY *smiles.*

DANNY. Three?

DANNY *goes in for another kiss.* LUKE *stops him.*

LUKE. Football.

That's what we can do. In the week. Help me get better at football.

DANNY. Do my best.

Kiss.

Week Four

VOICE ON RADIO. Man City, 0 – Tranny United, 1. Lesbian Rovers, 1 – Barely Athletic, 1.

DANNY and JOE *are sitting down.* VIV*'s stuck up a league table on a bit of A3.* GEOFF*'s holding the door open.*

LUKE moonwalks in. Everyone cheers.

VIV. I could kiss you, Luke.

GEOFF. I could bloody, bum you. In fact –

GEOFF grabs LUKE *and does some mime-bumming.* LUKE *laughs.*

LUKE. Only a goal, Geoff.

GEOFF. A beauty though.

JOE. Beardy, put him down.

GEOFF. Moonwalked into me.

LUKE sits down. DANNY *gets his arm round him, kisses him.* GEOFF *tuts.*

Bit much.

LUKE laughs.

LUKE. Might go for a shower.

VIV. No, sorry, need you all here.

JOE. Let him go, Viv. Just got us a point.

VIV. I know he did. And it's changed things for us, hasn't it? We need to just, take stock, as a team. It's important to share these moments together.

LUKE. Maybe have one later.

VIV. Here's how it stands. Four games down, two to play.

Top of the table: Lesbian Rovers. Played four, won two, drawn two, including us. Lost: zero games. Unbeaten. Eight well-deserved points. Think on.

If they somehow lost their next two games and we won our next two games we could still finish ahead of them, but maybe not ahead of whoever beat them, and from a personal point of view, I'd rather the lesbians won than Man City. Sort of think anywhere there's lesbians getting glory, I get a piece of it. By default. That's just how it works.

JOE. What about your trophy though?

VIV. Wait and see. Plans afoot. Thing to remember at this point is we've gone from five-nil last time we played the lesbians to one-all today. That speaks volumes doesn't it? Doesn't it? About the direction we're going in. About what's still to do.

JOE. It does.

VIV *points at the chart*.

VIV. Second place: seven points, Man City.

Second place? In the Hull Gay and Lesbian Five-a-side Football League? A bunch of smug, male-grooming, professional wankers. Fuck. Off. Sorry, Geoff, I know you're fond of them.

GEOFF. Fond-ish.

VIV. They've played four, won two, drawn one – Lesbians. And today they lost. Why did they lose? Cos they underestimated the fuck out of plucky relegation-zoners Tranny United. They thought they were better than them. We're not going to make that mistake in a fortnight's time. We were lucky last week, they were pissed and wearing stilettos, but they've obviously turned a corner and we can't be complacent. Can we?

GEOFF. No.

VIV. Before that though, there's the grudge match. I say we bring Man City down a peg or two. It won't be easy, we lost seven-nil last time. But I think we can all take a bit of inspiration from Tranny United. They started something we can finish, am I right?

DANNY. Course you are.

VIV. Good.

Third place: Barely Athletic. One win, one draw, two losses. Four points. Separated from fourth place Tranny United by a single point. That's all there is in it. Two games to go. What d'you reckon, lads?

VIV *gets a plastic bag. Takes the trophy out.*

I'm not asking you to come top of the league. I'll be delighted to watch Lesbian Rovers take this home with them. A victory for my people, if not for myself. I'm asking you…

VIV *takes out another, slightly smaller trophy.*

…to come second. Or possibly third.

VIV *gets another trophy out. This one is very small.*

That's what I'm asking.

Two more matches. Keep this up for two more matches and we get a trophy. I know you can do it.

LUKE. What about fourth?

VIV. Last you mean? No trophy for last.

DANNY. Unless you just buy one.

VIV. I won't be buying one.

A moment.

GEOFF. Really brings it home doesn't it. When you sort of. When you're just looking at them.

VIV. It's called 'visualisation', Geoff. Top coaching tip. For the under-nines.

GEOFF. Well, it's done the trick.

VIV. Good.

In that case…

VIV *holds her hand out*.

GEOFF. What?

VIV. Come on, love. Think we both know it's time. Hand it over.

GEOFF *holds on to his hat*.

Next week's important, Geoff. Man City play dirty, don't need any extra bits to grab.

GEOFF. Not ready. Take it off when I'm ready.

VIV. Never get anywhere in life with that on your head.

GEOFF. Well, you're wrong cos my life is going really well. That tagine was immense.

VIV. Paid Joe his rent yet?

GEOFF. Better than that. Got my song. For Pride.

Hopefully.

LUKE. Amazing.

DANNY. Play us it then.

VIV. Oh for –

DANNY. What?

VIV. I'm standing here trying to pave the way to a respectable finish for this team, you're all, the lot of you, you're… Where's the support, Danny? Doing this course but, when you get the chance to put it into practice – nothing. Don't you want to do well? Is that it? Don't you want this team to do well?

DANNY. I want this team to be fun. Room for, isn't there? Beardy's song. Luke's shower.

VIV. Sorry, Luke, you can have your shower.

LUKE. Maybe after the song.

GEOFF. Oh it's not ready yet, for –

DANNY. Go on, Beardy. Calm Viv down.

VIV. I don't need calming down, I need commitment.

JOE. Sing it.

GEOFF. Well. Okay but I should… Still in the process of sort of auditioning pieces so, this might not be perfect just. Danny said think gay. Uplifting and…

Worked out my intro an' all. Off to say, before I start: just so you know, not just singing this for me. Singing it for, for anyone who needs to hear it. Dedicated to, yeah. To a fairer world.

GEOFF *sings 'Go West'. Everyone joins in for the chorus.* GEOFF *peters out.*

JOE. Sounding good.

GEOFF. Really?

JOE. I was feeling it.

GEOFF. Hull's east though isn't it? Sing 'Go West' it's sort of like saying: go to Manchester. Or, you know, Hessle. That's not the message is it? Leave. And I know it's a classic but, yeah, just feels like a wasted opportunity. A bit. Cos, maybe not everyone wants to hear something, dunno, heartfelt or whatever but I reckon: someone does. And the, the poptastic ones, they'll be fine, go somewhere else for a shimmy. But that person, whoever it is, that person who's struggling, needs a bit of. Dunno. To take heart. I'm all they've got. And I should be… Cos, I know I'm not like a massive success or anything. Belting them out yesterday, opposite Lush – Half Man Half Biscuit, Arctic Monkeys, Hounds of Love – nothing. Made literally £1.37. And a Chewit. But, thing is, I'm also just: gay. Happy enough. In my skin. Got you lot. Loved. Reckon, get that across, someone takes a bit of heart from that. Job done.

VIV. I need a drink.

JOE. Right. Beardy?

VIV. Not sharing a car with that hat.

GEOFF. Off out anyway.

> JOE *and* VIV *leave*. LUKE *goes for his shower*. DANNY *sweeps*.

DANNY. Where you off?

GEOFF. Probably best not to…

DANNY. Geoff!

> GEOFF *smiles*.

GEOFF. Sean's. Round two.

DANNY. Viv'll be livid.

GEOFF. She'll never know.

DANNY. Course she will. Playing them next week.

GEOFF. I know I know but I just. Sent me this message this afternoon, one thing led to another.

DANNY. Shouldn't be reading his messages.

GEOFF. Nothing to read, just a picture. Of his –

DANNY. Yeah I can imagine.

GEOFF. Doubt it.

> What?

DANNY. I dunno. I just. Please don't.

GEOFF. What?

DANNY. You'll go meet him, something'll go wrong, make things more difficult next week. The match.

GEOFF. So?

DANNY. It's an important game.

GEOFF. Bad as Viv.

DANNY. Just want next week to go well. Extra well.

GEOFF. Why?

A moment.

DANNY. You can't tell the others?

GEOFF. Okay.

DANNY. Karen's coming to watch. Mark me. For my course.

GEOFF. What you on about?

DANNY. Part of my placement here. She wants to see a team that I've worked with and. I told her: come next week. Watch the match.

GEOFF. What d'you do that for?

DANNY. Cos, I dunno. Proud of everyone really. We are getting better. And I just think, all the other lads, they'll be dragging her to the some boring youth team, taking themselves dead serious. You lot though. Bit different. And, I don't want to tell the others cos, not good under pressure, are they, at all? Just want them to play normal and that but. Think, might be easier, next week, if you haven't pissed Sean off again. One less thing.

GEOFF. Honestly, Danny, you've got nothing to worry about. Absolutely nothing.

DANNY looks worried.

Just thought: bit of, you know. Romance. Might be nice. Eh? Eh?

DANNY (*smiling*). Sod off.

GEOFF. Come on then. Tell me.

DANNY. Just. Really like him. Makes me laugh and that.

GEOFF. Swoon.

DANNY. Like, I dunno. Saw him on Wednesday, met him after work for, we said we'd have like a little kick-about. And we did. And it was fun so, thought, do something else after. And I was like: what d'you feel like doing, Luke? Thinking sort of, drink, pictures… He goes: I've always wanted to do the Hull Fish Trail. You know all the, there's fish, in the pavement? Carvings. Follow them round, learn about Hull's fishy past. So that's. Suddenly I'm stood there, our first date, this hand, my hot chocolate, this hand, his hot chocolate, he's doing a brass rubbing of a mackerel. Amazing.

GEOFF. Sounds amazing.

DANNY. Thing is: I'm definitely not the weird one. Sometimes worry I'm a bit weird. Not with Luke. Just have fun, have a laugh. No pretending you're… Bit of a snog. Some fish. Lovely.

GEOFF. Did he think it was lovely?

DANNY *nods*.

DANNY. After Wednesday night we did Thursday night, Friday night, Saturday afternoon. It's all gone a bit *Notting Hill*.

GEOFF. Yeah. Four dates and you've managed: a snog. And some fish.

DANNY. Think it's all a bit new for him so. Yeah, just taking it slowly really. Just taking it really sort of, steady but.

GEOFF *looks at* DANNY.

What?

GEOFF. You haven't told him.

A moment.

DANNY. I will do.

GEOFF. Danny.

DANNY. I just, there hasn't been a, a good moment to…

GEOFF. There's never going to be a good moment. Is there? Just have to fucking, do it. Soon.

DANNY. Easy for you to say, isn't it? Skipping off to bloody, Sean, not a care in the world.

GEOFF. I'm sorry, I know it's. I do. But I just think you need
to… I mean I think he'll be, hopefully he'll be, you know.
But it is quite a big thing to, to get your head round and. I
just think: maybe, look after yourself. Tell him now, before
you get too sort of. Attached.

DANNY *bites his lip*.

Oh. How attached?

DANNY. Fairly attached.

GEOFF. Well then. Time to…

Promise me, Danny. Tonight. Promise me.

A moment.

DANNY. Thing is: I'm a bit…

Like there's this version in my head where, I tell him, sit him
down, tell him, he just sort of holds my hand goes: that's
fine. That is alright.

GEOFF. Exactly.

DANNY. But then there's… I dunno. What if he doesn't? If it's
not alright?

LUKE *comes in*.

GEOFF. Gutted. Thought I might catch a glimpse of this vest.

LUKE *is embarrassed*.

DANNY. When are you leaving, Geoff?

GEOFF. Now-ish. Be better if I was a bit late though really.
Don't want to seem desperate.

DANNY. Beardy, he summoned you with a picture of his cock.

GEOFF. I know: hot.

'Night, Luke.

LUKE. See you.

GEOFF (*to* DANNY). Give us a ring if you…

DANNY *nods*.

They wait for GEOFF *to leave*.

DANNY. Now.

They kiss.

LUKE. You're very kissy.

DANNY. That alright?

LUKE *nods*.

LUKE. Yeah.

Actually it's… Was thinking, Danny, in the shower.

DANNY. Oh right.

LUKE. Yeah, I was thinking this, you know, this taking it
slowly. Sort of thinking, like, that is a really good plan and
everything but, definitely but, I was wondering if just, if
maybe another good plan might be to sort of, yeah. Not take
things slowly?

DANNY. What d'you mean?

LUKE. Thing is: I really fancy you and you're, you're just,
you're… Wonder what the point is in sort of… Feel like,
really ready to… Yeah. Cos it's, I mean, don't know that
much about it but, you know. Heard it's. Fun?

DANNY. Yeah I heard that.

DANNY *looks worried*.

LUKE. But maybe you're not ready which is also fine. I'm
probably just, I'm being a knob aren't I? I am, I'm being a
massive div. Don't worry about it. No rush. No rush.

Or if you just don't want to, ever, that's fine too. I mean I get
it, I'm not like, like a sex god or anything am I? Far from it.
Far. From.

DANNY. Luke, I definitely want to.

LUKE. Oh that's brilliant.

DANNY. I just, there's some stuff we should probably, some stuff we need to, before we…

LUKE. Oh.

DANNY. I just, um. Never told anyone this before so… I mean Geoff knows but.

LUKE *sits down*. DANNY *holds his hand*.

LUKE. Whatever it is, it's, I'm sure it's…

DANNY. Maybe easier if I just…

Well.

You know how Beardy's a bit of a. I dunno. Gets around a bit.

LUKE *nods*.

Well, not now, he's careful now but when I first knew him, he was quite. Reckless or… He'd just go out, get off his face, go home with anyone and. Yeah. I was a bit worried he wasn't… Cos sometimes he couldn't remember, sometimes, what he'd done and that. If he'd been safe or… So, couple of years ago now, I just told him straight out he needed to get tested. He started sort of panicking and I said in that case he definitely needed to get tested but if he's frightened I'll go with him, get tested too.

LUKE. Be his wingman.

DANNY. Exactly. Cos I was, nothing to worry about really. Been going out with this lad who, we'd been together sort of six months, he was at uni here and. It was pretty sort of, solid so, you know.

But then, turned out, he hadn't been quite as, honest or. Careful, as I thought. This lad. Anyway, I got tested, Geoff got tested. Geoff had chlamydia, gutted but, you know. Sortable. And I had, yeah. I had, um.

A moment.

LUKE. You had…?

Deep breath.

DANNY. I had HIV.

I've got HIV.

A moment.

LUKE. What?

DANNY. I know it sounds –

LUKE (*quiet*). Shit, Danny.

LUKE *stands up.*

DANNY. Luke.

LUKE. Why didn't you tell me?

DANNY. Quite a big thing to, quite hard to, to tell someone.

LUKE. Quite a big thing not to tell someone.

DANNY. Telling you now.

LUKE. Yeah. I just.

DANNY. Luke, calm down. Sit down.

LUKE. I just, I need a minute to. No, actually. Think I need more than a minute.

LUKE *gets his stuff.*

We should talk about this, another time.

A moment.

DANNY. Yeah get lost then.

LUKE. What?

DANNY. Sorry this is so hard. For you.

LUKE. Should've told me at the start.

DANNY. So you could leg it then? Save some time.

LUKE. Danny.

DANNY. Got everything?

LUKE *stands there. Upset.*

(*Quietly.*) Fuck off, Luke.

LUKE *tries to go. Struggles with the door. Opens it. Leaves.*

DANNY *sweeps, angry and upset.*

Week Five

VOICE ON RADIO. Lesbian Rovers, 5 – Tranny United, 4. Man City, 6 – Barely Athletic, 0.

GEOFF *is sitting down, leaning his head back and holding a tissue against his bloody nose.* JOE *and* DANNY *and* VIV *are sitting around him.* JOE *has a loo roll.* DANNY *looks annoyed.*

VIV. Just keep pinching.

GEOFF (*to* DANNY). Sorry.

JOE. Maybe try leaning forward?

GEOFF. Pardon?

JOE. Think it's meant to help if you… Or, dunno actually, might pour out faster.

GEOFF. Don't think it could pour out any faster.

VIV. Well then.

GEOFF *leans forward.*

GEOFF. Still pinching am I, Joe?

VIV. Fuck's sake, Beardy. Yes still pinching. Do not stop pinching till I say you can stop pinching.

GEOFF. Feel shit we had to stop the match.

VIV. Not your fault was it? Bloody, Sean. He's a headcase.

GEOFF. Probably just an accident.

DANNY. I dunno. Looked pretty pleased with himself.

GEOFF. That's just his face.

VIV. Smug bastard.

GEOFF. I'm so sorry, Danny.

VIV. Will you stop apologising? Tell him, Danny. Not your fault.

DANNY. It is his fault.

Told you not to see Sean, still went and did it, next thing: possible broken nose.

So it is his fault.

VIV. Fuck's sake, Beardy.

GEOFF. Nothing happened. Stood me up actually.

VIV. What's his problem then?

GEOFF. I honestly don't know, Viv. All I did, I marked him quite tightly and sang a small amount of Enya. Think it was Enya. Might've been T'Pau. Didn't think he'd heard but then out of nowhere started tackling me. In the face. With his elbow.

I'm sorry, Danny.

DANNY. Don't.

VIV. What you apologising to him for?

If you've fucked it up, fucked it up for everyone.

Luke misses his bus, he's a div who lives in the middle of nowhere, nothing we can do about that. Also, he gets special treatment cos he's new and Danny loves him. Bloody, Butterfingers here in goal, that's just Joe. We play round it. But taunting the opposition with Enya. Possibly T'Pau. Not helpful. Thankfully Tranny United lost an' all, and we've still got a match to go but. Honestly. It should not be this hard to get a very small trophy. It really shouldn't.

DANNY. We'll buy you a trophy, Viv. Don't worry about your trophy.

VIV. Yeah great, why don't we all just buy ourselves a trophy instead of getting a boost from actually winning one?

GEOFF. You did buy them.

VIV. Tissue swap.

>   VIV *clamps new loo roll on* GEOFF's *nose.*

GEOFF. Ow.

VIV. Shut up and pinch.

DANNY. You weren't that helpful either, Viv.

VIV. Sticking up for him.

DANNY. By calling the ref a –

VIV. He is one. I'd do it again.

DANNY. You better not.

JOE. It would be better, Viv, if you didn't.

VIV. Be better if you didn't let six goals in but I'm not going on about it.

DANNY. How's your nose?

>   GEOFF *takes the tissue away.*

GEOFF. I'm being very brave but it does hurt quite a lot.

DANNY. Get a can out the vending machine. Hold against it. Something cold.

GEOFF. Thank you.

>   DANNY *leaves.*

VIV. What is his problem today?

GEOFF. Don't, Viv.

VIV. Needs his sense of humour testing.

JOE. Think you've probably tested it quite a lot.

>   VIV *laughs.*

VIV. Tested the ref's.

>   JOE *smiles.*

GEOFF. It's not funny.

VIV. I know but. Done now. Nothing I can do about it is there?

And at least we bloody, turned up. Luke's not getting sulked at. If he'd texted me to say he'd missed his bus I'd've been on the phone doing my nut but Danny's all, not his fault, let's not talk about it.

Anyway. Danny's the one going on the whole time how it doesn't matter if you win or not, just enjoy it. Getting the best out of people.

GEOFF. We didn't though, did we? Enjoy it. That wasn't our best. I'm haemorrhaging, you got booked for bollocking the ref and we had to stop the match. Joe's the only one who's reliable.

JOE. Not reliable, Geoff. I'm shit.

GEOFF. Reliably shit.

VIV. I've said: all we have to do next week is beat Tranny United. It'll either be easy or hard depending if they're sober. But it's do-able. This week was a cock-up. End of. Doesn't matter.

GEOFF *sighs*.

What?

GEOFF. Matters to Danny.

VIV. He's only moping cos Luke's not here.

GEOFF. He isn't.

VIV. Course he is.

GEOFF. He really isn't.

JOE. Is something up, Beardy?

GEOFF. What you on about?

JOE. You just. You don't seem your usual happy-go-lucky self.

GEOFF. It's just concussion.

JOE. Sure?

GEOFF. Yeah.

JOE. Really?

GEOFF. Nothing's going on. And even if something was going on – which it isn't – even if something was going on, I wouldn't be allowed to say, cos I promised Danny.

VIV. Oh fuck's sake, Beardy.

GEOFF. What?

VIV. That – I've got a secret, can't tell you but I've got one – that is like my number-one pet hate.

GEOFF. Thought your number-one pet hate was halloumi.

VIV. It's a draw. Between the two.

Tell us.

GEOFF. Ask Danny.

VIV. We're asking you.

GEOFF. And I am sworn to secrecy so.

JOE. What's it about?

VIV. I'm not playing twenty questions, Joe. Tell us.

A moment.

Tell us or I'll honk your nose.

GEOFF. About his course.

He was getting assessed today. That's why Karen was there. To see how he's done, coaching-wise. Assistant-coaching-wise.

A moment.

VIV. Fuck.

GEOFF. Yeah.

VIV. Fucking hell. Shit.

JOE. Might be alright.

VIV. Don't be a knob, Joe, it's a disaster. Me gobbing off at the ref, Beardy scrapping, you – you might as well have sat down. Least you'd've blocked a few. And Luke, missing his bloody bus – what was he thinking? Must've known about it.

GEOFF. Don't think so.

VIV. He must've.

GEOFF *shakes his head*.

Something going on there an' all?

GEOFF. Course not. And if there was, I wouldn't be allowed to say.

JOE. I'm lost.

GEOFF. Can we just, can we talk about something else? Talk about next week or something.

VIV. Well, we can't really can we? I mean, is Luke even coming next week? Have we got a team?

GEOFF *shakes his head*.

Typical.

JOE. Don't get mad.

VIV. I just think it's… Like we've all had a go at Geoff for shagging Sean. Turns out it's Danny who's. In the end. Hops into bed with Luke, messes it up, now we've got no team.

GEOFF. That isn't what happened. Anyway let's just…

DANNY *comes back. Gives* GEOFF *a can.* GEOFF *holds it against his nose*.

Everyone is quiet.

DANNY. What's going on?

JOE. We're sorry for… Didn't mean to show you up. In front of Karen.

DANNY *huffs*.

DANNY (*to* GEOFF). Not your day is it?

Tell you what: you lot clear up tonight. I'm off home.

JOE. Danny.

DANNY *chucks the keys at* JOE.

DANNY. See. You can catch.

JOE. Don't leave now, when you're mad with us.

DANNY. Well, I am doing.

JOE. Might not be as bad as you think.

DANNY. I'm pretty sure I've failed.

GEOFF. You won't've done.

DANNY. Karen asked if I was taking the piss.

VIV. Need you here, Danny. Got to sort out next week.

Still got Tranny United to beat haven't we? Without Luke by the sound of it an' all.

DANNY. Beardy.

GEOFF. I just, I crumbled.

VIV. The point is: I refuse to finish this league as a four-a-side football team. What sort of knobheads play four-a-side football? Not us. We're better than that. So, yeah. This tiff you've had with Luke, is it mendable?

GEOFF. Viv.

VIV. Only asking.

GEOFF. Wasn't a tiff.

VIV. Mendable then. Perfect.

DANNY. Not mendable.

VIV. It better be.

Look, I'm sorry it didn't go well in front of Karen but there's nothing we can do about it now is there? The only thing we can sort is next week. And thing is, Danny: that is what coaches do. They sort next week. They're gutted, they put it behind them and they sort next week. And if you can't do that you probably shouldn't be passing your course anyway.

GEOFF. Viv!

VIV. Well, it's true. Cos, thing is: we started this as a team. The rules are: finish it as a team. Can't change your mind halfway through, that's not… A team is: you work with what you've got. I could've looked at you lot, week one, stood you all in a row gone: wow. What a bunch of fucking mop-ups.

DANNY. You did.

VIV. Didn't stop me though. Cos you're my team. My people. The ones who turned up. Cos, asked everyone from the pub, I did, no one gave a shit apart from you and Beardy. My two best lads. Forced Joe, he came in the end, even though he's straight and, and miserable. Luke turns up from your poster. And that's a team. And it's not failing if we haven't got a trophy, I couldn't give a shit any more. They were dead cheap anyway. But it's, it does feel like failing if we haven't got a team. It just does.

DANNY. Have to fail then cos. Yeah. Me or Luke. Not both.

VIV. Oh get lost then, moody.

Your attitude's shit.

DANNY *leaves*.

GEOFF. Good work, Viv. Kick him when he's down.

VIV. All he's got to do is play nicely next week and it'll be fine. I've got half a mind to ring Luke up, give him a bollocking an' all.

What?

GEOFF. Please don't do that.

VIV. Got a better idea have you?

GEOFF. I do as it goes.

> GEOFF *grins*.

> Leave everything to me.

VIV. And watch it go to shit even more?

JOE. Viv.

VIV. I'm the only thing holding this lot together.

GEOFF. I know, this is my fault. I know. Sang 'China in Your Hand', accidentally dismantled a football team. So I get it, I'm a risk. But also, I know I can make it all better, and I really really want to. I'm thinking: talk to Karen, explain what happened, get her to be a bit kind with her marking. Reckon I'm charming enough, get him a pass at least. Maybe aim for merit or distinction. Then, moving quickly, guilt-trip Danny into speaking to Luke, at the very least a text, invite him back next week, no hard feelings and that. This lays the groundwork for a trip to the library. Tell Luke how much we all miss him. He pops up next week. This is do-able. Definitely sortable but. Might be easier if you just trust me. Rather than ringing people up and bollocking them. It might come to that but. Let me try first.

> *A moment.*

VIV. I give up.

GEOFF. Brilliant!

> Full set next week, I promise.

> GEOFF *leaves*.

> VIV *sits down*.

> JOE *gets the brush, sweeps one-handed*.

VIV. Joe, seriously. Who sweeps with one hand?

> VIV *takes the brush off* JOE. *Sweeps*.

> What?

JOE. Nothing.

VIV. What you looking like that for?

JOE. I'm not, just… What you said before. You don't have to hold it all together, Viv. Just so you know. It's fine to have a bit of… I mean everyone has… You could say, you could tell me, if you're, yeah. If you're struggling.

VIV sweeps.

VIV. I'm a coper, Joe.

JOE. Not sure you are, Viv.

VIV. Well, I am. Keep looking forwards.

JOE. There's a difference though isn't there? Looking forwards is, but. Flinging yourself head-first into stuff, one thing after another, that's… Never have chance to. Like, next week, when this is finished, what'll you…?

VIV. Got a pub to run haven't I? That doesn't stop.

What?

JOE. Just think, if you wanted to… Just go. Spend some time there. Think and. Remember. Could just come with me one day. Cos, think you might be surprised. Doesn't feel how you… People wandering round, kids in buggies, trees and that. More alive really. Than you think.

VIV sweeps.

VIV. Got enough on sorting out this lot.

JOE. Beardy says he'll sort it, he'll sort it.

VIV snorts.

Give him a chance, Viv. You have a week off. A week off all of us. Sit down with Lisa. Watch some telly. Please. For me.

A moment.

VIV. Have you got the keys? I'm all done.

Week Six

VOICE ON RADIO. Lesbian Rovers, 3 – Man City, 2. Tranny
United, 1 – Barely Athletic, 0.

Everyone's there.

GEOFF. Not a trophy, I know but. And obviously it would've
been better if we'd beaten Tranny United. That'd be the sort
of Hollywood ending. Think the sight of that lad in a leopard-
print miniskirt slipping a cheeky ball between Joe's legs
seconds before the final whistle is something we'll all
remember for a very long time but. Thing about us, what I've
learned about us: we're fucking good losers. We really are.
And, just thought, since we're all here – some more keen than
others, obvs, but – just thought: something to put behind your
bar. For putting up with us. From everyone. Well, Joe got
them but. From the garage but. We got them too, in spirit.

GEOFF gives VIV some unimpressive flowers.

And we promise: next season right, next season we'll go one
better. Next season we're aiming for third.

VIV is touched.

VIV. Thought you wouldn't want to.

GEOFF. What?

VIV. Thought this'd be it, footy-wise.

Thought I'd have to go ask the lesbians if they'll have me
back.

GEOFF. They wouldn't.

VIV. I know.

A moment.

Here's to next season then.

One condition: someone else has to be in charge.

VIV *takes her top off. Holds it out for* DANNY. DANNY *looks lost.*

Head coach Danny. Need to swap shirts.

DANNY. Do we?

A moment.

Says Viv on it.

VIV (*smiles*). What an honour for you.

DANNY *smiles.*

DANNY. Cheers.

They swap shirts.

VIV. Got to buck your ideas up a bit, mind. Karen scraped you through this time, might not be so lucky next time. And she's right, got to take charge a bit more. Got to really grab this team by the bollocks and. Yeah.

DANNY. Do my best.

JOE. Pub?

GEOFF. Think it's time for your bus, Luke.

LUKE. Oh. Yes. It is.

LUKE *puts his coat on.*

VIV. Come for a drink tonight. All of us. Together.

GEOFF. You can't, can you, Luke?

LUKE. Not really.

JOE. Yorkshire puddings?

LUKE. Um, no, actually. Wheel of sausage.

VIV. What?

LUKE. My mum got sick of, well, so. Taken my dad on this cookery course. Long weekend. You sort of, you stay in this big house, someone posh tells you how to whisk. They reckon it'll sort the Yorkshire puddings out. Doubt it but. Yeah. I'm just fending for myself really. Went to Tesco's, got a crusty roll and a wheel of sausage. Can't wait.

But anyway, better. Better bus.

VIV. One of us can give you a lift back. Come. Team drink.

GEOFF. Give him a break, Viv. The man's got a bus to catch. And I can't come either tonight so: no point really, is there?

VIV. Come for a bit, Beardy.

GEOFF. I can't, Viv. Still haven't got my song. Cos this week has just been non-stop, sorting stuff out, had to put all thoughts of Hull Pride glory on the back burner, which I don't mind, at all – I live to give but. Suddenly: audition's tomorrow. No song. And it might be alright, might be a disaster but I just think I need to really knuckle down tonight, rack my brains, investigate the jukebox in my soul. I just, I owe it to myself really. And to Hull.

Luke, you really had better…

VIV. See you soon then, love.

LUKE *gets the door right*.

LUKE (*quietly*). Did it.

GEOFF *gives him a thumbs-up. He leaves*.

VIV *and* JOE *look at* DANNY.

DANNY. What?

VIV. Walk him to the bus stop at least.

DANNY *shakes his head*.

DANNY. We're just mates. Decided.

JOE. Who decided?

DANNY. I decided. And it's, yeah. Good decision.

I should get cleared up and that. You lot head off. Catch you up.

JOE. Are you sure, Danny? Cos, to me, you seem like… Both of you. Seem like…

DANNY. I better…

DANNY *sweeps*. JOE *stays put*.

JOE. D'you know how I met Julie? Can I tell you?

DANNY *stops sweeping*.

Just in a pub. Old Town. Went out with my mate Tony – he's in prison now – made a pact, that night, we'd both ask someone out. Cos it'd been a while. For both of us. It was one of them nights where, pissing it down, we both just sat there feeling damp, watching nothing happen. But there was this one girl who we both liked. Dead classy. She'd got like a dress, face, everything. Shouted last orders, thought one of us better have a go, ask her out. Tossed a coin to decide. I lost. Got chatting to Julie instead.

Not much of a start. She was a bit pissed, forgot my name. Kept just calling me British Gas.

But it was everything after that, you know. Mattered. Just ordinary stuff. Trying. Having a laugh. Fucking up. Ploughing on. Arguing, not arguing. It's boring except it's not boring cos inside you it's all bloody, swirling round all, massive and, and messy. Brilliant.

Remember thinking: I am quite an average man. Never thought I'd feel…

VIV*'s a bit upset*. JOE *hasn't noticed*.

Thing is, Danny: shit start – still a start. Cos not everyone finds someone. Do they? Someone to… So if you're, if you're getting there – and you are, Danny. If you're getting there, think maybe just: count yourself lucky.

I always did anyway.

VIV *sniffs into her flowers*.

Oh shit.

VIV. You're alright, I'm being… Shouldn't've.

JOE. Sorry.

VIV. Don't be daft.

I remember actually, day after, she came downstairs, beaming. I said: come on then, what's his name? She goes: not a clue, but he reckons he can mend the boiler.

JOE *smiles*.

JOE. Pub?

VIV. Maybe.

JOE. Beardy's round. Kidding.

VIV. Thing is: yeah.

Just thinking…

Got these.

Thing is: I'm not like a very floral person really. Am I though?

Wondered if, would you mind if. Just stopped off on the way and… Come with me. Just a few minutes.

A moment.

JOE. Sure?

VIV *nods*.

Right then.

Catch up with you lads a bit later.

VIV *and* JOE *leave*.

DANNY *sweeps*. GEOFF *watches*.

GEOFF. Went to the library yesterday.

DANNY. Don't start.

GEOFF. He was just stood there looking at the community noticeboard.

Poster's still up. Glitter glue.

DANNY. Geoff.

Look, I'm glad this happened cos. I told him and, you were right. Things aren't a hundred per cent wrong. I know I can do it again now so. I'm glad. But just, not with Luke.

GEOFF. He was just surprised.

DANNY. Maybe.

GEOFF. He's nineteen, Danny. Lives in a village. Struggles with doors. Just trying to get his head round it. He's there now.

DANNY. I just, I look at him and I see him legging it. When the one thing I needed him to do was sort of, not leg it. Needed him to stay.

GEOFF *pulls a face*.

What?

GEOFF. Nothing. You should have a shower.

DANNY. What?

GEOFF. Just a nice, a relaxing shower.

DANNY. Got to clear up.

GEOFF. I'll clear up.

DANNY. You never clear up.

GEOFF. I will tonight just. You go through there, for a bit.

DANNY. Right, what is going on?

GEOFF. I just, I've slightly misjudged things.

It's nothing bad. Or actually, is it bad? Yeah, it is really, probably. Bad.

GEOFF *looks under one of the benches*. DANNY *follows his gaze*. LUKE*'s bag is hidden there*.

Told him to forget his bag and then come back for it. So you could chat. Now. Without everyone else… Things were going so well getting the team back together, got overexcited. Started to think of myself as a sort of Cupid figure.

GEOFF *picks up* LUKE*'s bag from under one of the benches. Looks at his watch*.

But, um, yeah. Be here in about a minute so.

You just go. I'll explain.

DANNY. It's fine.

GEOFF. Or we'll both talk to him.

DANNY. I'll talk to him.

GEOFF. No need.

DANNY. You go for a shower.

GEOFF. I've had one this week.

DANNY. Beardy.

DANNY *gives* GEOFF *a look*. GEOFF *goes for a shower*. DANNY *sits, holding* LUKE*'s bag*.

LUKE *comes in. Nervous*.

LUKE. Um.

Geoff's idea. Sorry.

DANNY *passes* LUKE *his bag*.

DANNY. Still get your bus if you run.

LUKE. Yeah.

LUKE *just stands there*.

I just, I would, if it's alright, I would like to talk to you for a minute, Danny, if that's…?

DANNY. I've got to sweep up really.

LUKE. I'll help.

DANNY. Only one brush.

LUKE. Danny, please.

DANNY. What?

LUKE. I know I fucked up, Danny. I know I did. You said it and I just, I panicked –

DANNY. I noticed.

LUKE. But then, as soon as I was the other side of the door, honestly, I was just like: Luke, you absolute idiot. Don't leave him. Get back in there. Hug him. But I was scared I'd get it wrong, say the wrong thing cos, I didn't know what to say. So I didn't. But I wish I had done. I really wish I had done so. Just thought, today, just wanted to check really. Just – and it's fine to say no but, just in case: wondered if we could maybe sort of, yeah, have another go? Cos, yeah. I'd love that to be honest.

DANNY*'s face is hard to read.*

Don't say no yet, not yet, just. One second cos… There's some stuff I should've, ages ago but. I just, I didn't so… Um. Yeah.

LUKE *looks in his diary. Finds the page.*

'Porridge boiled over in the microwave this morning. It is actually quite a tricky stain to clean so I missed the 77. Got the 75 instead. It goes via Burstwick and Holderness Road. Got in late.'

DANNY. Luke, you did this.

LUKE. Just, just bear with me. Please.

'Spent two hours trying to reshelve Mills and Boons without disturbing a sleeping tramp. Jacket potato for lunch.

That lad came in again this afternoon. Brought a poster.

And I wanted to just. I dunno.

He is the most beautiful thing I've ever seen in Adidas
trackies. When he's there I just want to shout my life is
boring please be in it. Across the library. Just shout. I nearly
did today but then I thought it could go either way so I just
breathed really hard instead. Probably sounds daft but he
smells immense and now there's little particles of him up my
nose. Which is a bit like having sex maybe. I dunno.

You know when you fancy someone so much you could just
vom? Just throw up your whole life in front of him like: have
it. Please. Let's go on adventures, you can meet my nan. It's
like that. But also a bit like having a stroke. In a good way.
Heart and head and, you know. Limbs. And when he leaves
you're just like: numb.

I want to wear his jumpers. Doubt they'd fit but.

Wish I was braver. Wish I was better at football.'

LUKE *stops reading*.

Honestly, Danny, there's no one in this world I'd rather put a
condom on than you.

LUKE *fishes in his pocket*.

Got ribbed, extra-safe. Pineapple.

DANNY. Pineapple?

LUKE. Thought: exotic.

DANNY *smiles*.

DANNY. Just be two people. Being careful. Seeing how they
get on.

LUKE *nods*.

Your place or mine?

LUKE *smiles*.

LUKE. What about sweeping?

DANNY. Geoff'll manage.

DANNY *gets his stuff.*

Come on, you.

DANNY *moves* LUKE *towards the door.*

LUKE. Just a sec.

LUKE *writes something on a page of his diary, tears it out and leaves it on top of* GEOFF's *guitar.*

They leave, holding hands.

GEOFF *comes back in from the shower.*

Looks at the bit of paper. Smiles.

Picks up his guitar.

GEOFF. Just so you know, not just singing this for me. Singing it for, for anyone who needs to hear it. Dedicated to, yeah. To a fairer world.

GEOFF *sings 'You'll Never Walk Alone'. Finishes.*

Takes his hat off. Holds it high.

End of play.

Other Titles in this Series

A Nick Hern Book

Jumpers for Goalposts first published in Great Britain as a paperback original
in 2013 by Nick Hern Books Limited, The Glasshouse, 49a Goldhawk Road,
London W12 8QP, in association with Paines Plough, Watford Palace Theatre
and Hull Truck Theatre

Cover image by Graham Michael
Cover designed by Ned Hoste, 2H

Typeset by Nick Hern Books, London
Printed in the UK by CPI Group (UK) Ltd

A CIP catalogue record for this book is available from the British Library

ISBN 978 1 84842 326 8